George W. Bush

The Presidents of the United States

George Washington
1789–1797

John Adams
1797–1801

Thomas Jefferson
1801–1809

James Madison
1809–1817

James Monroe
1817–1825

John Quincy Adams
1825–1829

Andrew Jackson
1829–1837

Martin Van Buren
1837–1841

William Henry Harrison
1841

John Tyler
1841–1845

James Polk
1845–1849

Zachary Taylor
1849–1850

Millard Fillmore
1850–1853

Franklin Pierce
1853–1857

James Buchanan
1857–1861

Abraham Lincoln
1861–1865

Andrew Johnson
1865–1869

Ulysses S. Grant
1869–1877

Rutherford B. Hayes
1877–1881

James Garfield
1881

Chester Arthur
1881–1885

Grover Cleveland
1885–1889

Benjamin Harrison
1889–1893

Grover Cleveland
1893–1897

William McKinley
1897–1901

Theodore Roosevelt
1901–1909

William H. Taft
1909–1913

Woodrow Wilson
1913–1921

Warren Harding
1921–1923

Calvin Coolidge
1923–1929

Herbert Hoover
1929–1933

Franklin D. Roosevelt
1933–1945

Harry Truman
1945–1953

Dwight Eisenhower
1953–1961

John F. Kennedy
1961–1963

Lyndon B. Johnson
1963–1969

Richard Nixon
1969–1974

Gerald Ford
1974–1977

Jimmy Carter
1977–1981

Ronald Reagan
1981–1989

George H. W. Bush
1989–1993

William J. Clinton
1993–2001

George W. Bush
2001–2009

Barack Obama
2009–

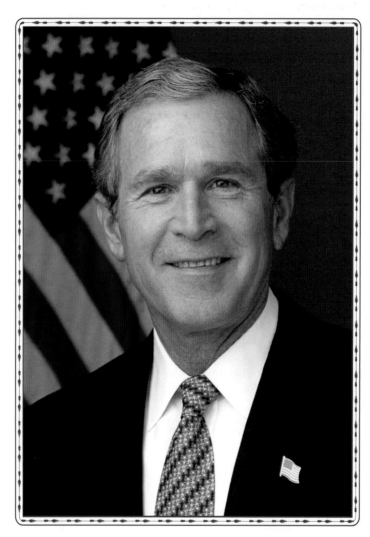

GEORGE W. BUSH

MICHAEL BURGAN WEST BEND LIBRARY

mc Marshall Cavendish
Benchmark
New York

Website: www.marshallcavendish.us

This publication represents the opinions and views of the author based on Michael Burgan's personal experience, knowledge, and research. The information in this book serves as a general guide only. The author and publisher have used their best efforts in preparing this book and disclaim liability rising directly and indirectly from the use and application of this book.

Other Marshall Cavendish Offices:
Marshall Cavendish International (Asia) Private Limited, 1 New Industrial Road, Singapore 536196 • Marshall Cavendish International (Thailand) Co Ltd. 253 Asoke, 12th Flr, Sukhumvit 21 Road, Klongtoey Nua, Wattana, Bangkok 10110, Thailand • Marshall Cavendish (Malaysia) Sdn Bhd, Times Subang, Lot 46, Subang Hi-Tech Industrial Park, Batu Tiga, 40000 Shah Alam, Selangor Darul Ehsan, Malaysia

Marshall Cavendish is a trademark of Times Publishing Limited

All websites were available and accurate when this book was sent to press.

Library of Congress Cataloging-in-Publication Data

Burgan, Michael.
George W. Bush / Michael Burgan.
p. cm. — (Presidents and their times)
Summary: "Provides comprehensive information on President George W. Bush and places him within his historical and cultural context. Also explored are the formative events of his times and how he responded"—Provided by publisher.
Includes bibliographical references and index.
ISBN 978-1-60870-184-1
1. Bush, George W. (George Walker), 1946—Juvenile literature. 2. Presidents—United States—Biography—Juvenile literature. I. Title.

E903.B8624 2012
973.931092—dc 22
[B]2010014801

Editor: Christine Florie
Publisher: Michelle Bisson
Art Director: Anahid Hamparian
Series Designer: Alex Ferrari

Photo research by Marybeth Kavanagh

Cover photo by Chip Somodevilla/Getty Images

The photographs in this book are used by permission and through the courtesy of: *Getty Images*: Mark Wilson, 6; Darren McCollester/Newsmakers, 12; Timothy A. Clary/AFP, 33; Don Emmert/AFP, 39; Robert King/Newsmakers, 41; Tim Sloan/AFP, 46, 67; CNN, 58; Stephen Jaffe/AFP, 60; Charles Ommanney, 65; Jay Mallin/Bloomberg, 72; Paul J. Richards/AFP, 76; *George Bush Presidential Library and Museum*: 9, 10, 14, 19; *AP Photo*: 47; Sky Gilbar, 17; J. Scott Applewhite, 22; Eric Draper, 35; Paul Morse/White House, 44; INA, 55; *SuperStock*: IndexStock, 26; Photononstop, 50; Science Faction, 69; *The Image Works*: Bob Daemmrich, 27, 29, 63; Tannen Maury, 36; Michael Siluk, 78; *Corbis*: Mark Bryan Makela/In Pictures, 83; Tannen Maury/Pool, 84; *White House*: Eric Draper: 3, 87

Printed in Malaysia
1 3 5 6 4 2

CONTENTS

J
973.931
B 91

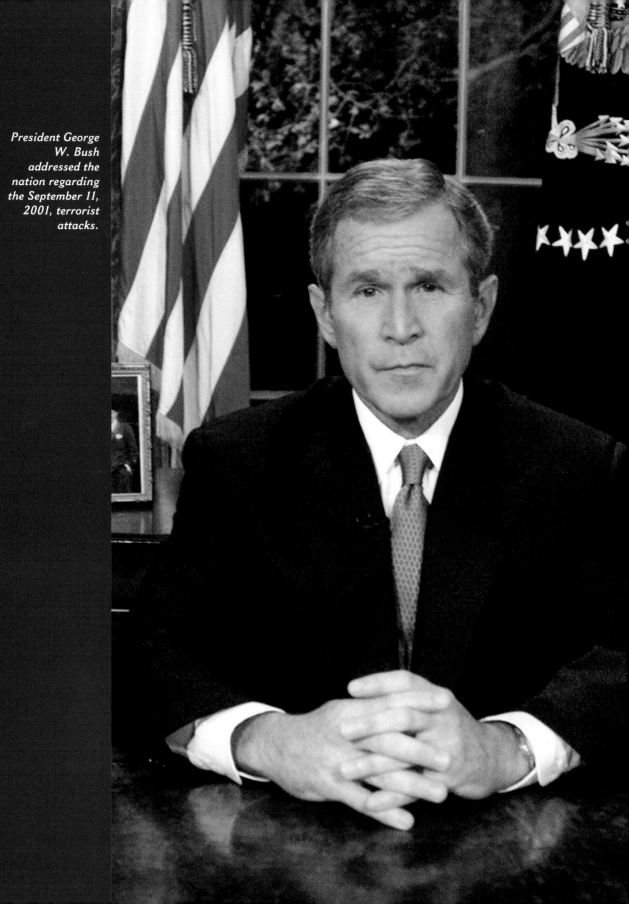

President George W. Bush addressed the nation regarding the September 11, 2001, terrorist attacks.

Becoming the "War President"

One

On the morning of September 11, 2001, President George W. Bush arrived at Emma E. Booker Elementary School in Sarasota, Florida. The forty-third president was about to meet some of the school's second graders. Shortly before 9 a.m., one of Bush's aides told him that a plane had crashed into one of the two towers at New York City's World Trade Center. The president had once flown military jets for the National Guard. He told an aide the pilot must have made a bad error. "You just don't just hit a building like that," he said.

Minutes later, inside the classroom, Bush sat with the students. Another aide came to the president's side and whispered in his ear: "A second plane hit the second tower. America is under attack." If that were true, Bush would soon have to play one of the most important roles for a U.S. president—commander in chief of the armed forces.

As the morning went on, Bush learned that two more planes had been hijacked. One slammed into the Pentagon, headquarters for the U.S. military in Washington, D.C. Another crashed in a Pennsylvania field. Its target had been another important building in Washington, D.C. A group of Arab men with extreme religious beliefs had taken over the planes to use them as weapons. The attacks reflected anger with the United States and its policies overseas. Bush soon learned that terrorist leader Osama bin Laden was behind the attacks, which had killed almost three thousand people.

On the night of September 11, Bush spoke to the nation. "Freedom itself was attacked this morning by faceless cowards. And freedom will be defended." Bush soon ordered an invasion of Afghanistan, where bin Laden was living and training terrorists. A year later, the president and his advisers were planning to invade Iraq as well, fearing it, too, would help terrorists attack the United States and its allies.

During his eight years as president, George W. Bush faced many crises and worked on important issues. But the wars in Afghanistan and Iraq took most of his energy and attention. He became, as he said, a "war president." For a time, Americans supported Bush in what he called a war on terrorism. The president and his advisers were sure they knew what to do. But they made mistakes along the way, and by 2008 some Americans grew tired of the wars, which were costly and did not seem close to ending. Bush left office with few Americans still supporting him.

A Powerful Family

Years before, George Walker Bush had seen his father, George Herbert Walker Bush, lead a war against Iraq. The elder Bush had been elected the forty-first president of the United States in 1988. The two men were only the second father and son to hold that office (John Adams, who served between 1797 and 1801, and his son John Quincy Adams [1825–1829] were the first).

George W. was a teenager when his father first entered politics. The family tradition of public service went back even further. Prescott Bush, George's grandfather, served as a U.S.

senator from Connecticut from 1952 to 1963, after a successful career in banking. On both sides of his family, the future forty-third president had ties to wealthy and important people.

George W. Bush was born on July 6, 1946, in New Haven, Connecticut, where his father was a student at Yale, one of the country's best universities. Rather than beginning college right after high school, the elder Bush

George W. Bush was born in New Haven, Connecticut, to Barbara and George H. W. Bush on July 6, 1946.

had served in World War II, which ended in 1945. As a navy pilot, he fought bravely, winning a medal for his service.

When young George was almost two years old, his parents, George and Barbara, moved to Texas. Rather than following Prescott Bush into banking, George H. W. Bush hoped to make money drilling for oil. With help from his family and his father's friends, the young navy veteran began a successful business career. He and his family settled in Midland, Texas, in the heart of the state's oil country.

In Texas, young George was soon joined by a sister, Robin, and during the 1950s, four more Bush children followed. The family suffered a deep loss in 1953, when Robin died of leukemia, a form of cancer. George W. was just seven at the time, and he saw how much his sister's death affected his parents, especially his mother. He tried to tell jokes and cheer her up. Young George would continue to play this role as he grew older. He enjoyed making others laugh. His easy way of getting along with most people would help him when he entered politics.

School Days

Through the 1950s George went to Midland schools. In junior high school he was a good student and popular with others, though he struck some people as arrogant. He learned to play baseball from his father, who had been a star on his college team. In 1959 the Bushes left Midland and moved to Houston, where George began high school. In 1961 his parents sent him to Andover, Massachusetts, home of Phillips Academy. The private high school was one of the best in the country, and his father had gone there, too.

His classmates nicknamed George "the Lip" because he talked so much and sometimes spoke harshly of others. He struggled for a time with both math and English, and sometimes he worried about flunking out of school and disappointing his parents. But he managed to earn average grades and became involved in sports. He organized several teams to play stickball, a form of baseball. During his senior year, he served as a cheerleader for the football team. With his high energy and knack for having fun, George became popular at Andover.

The Bush children raise a flag in the yard of their Midland, Texas, home.

"Baby Boomer" President

George W. Bush was one of about 76 million Americans born between 1946 and 1964, the so-called baby boomers. Most were the children of Americans who had fought during World War II. The war, and the bad economic times before it called the Great Depression, had slowed population growth in the United States. The baby boom era saw an explosive rise in the country's birthrate. Bush and other baby boomers grew up when millions of Americans were leaving cities to live in suburbs and it was becoming common across the country for families to own television sets. The boomers' parents, on the whole, earned better wages than earlier generations of Americans. As the boomers became teens, they had money to spend on music, films, clothes, and other items. Companies began to pay attention to their interests and needs. Bush was the second baby boomer president, after Bill Clinton.

But few of his classmates imagined he would one day enter politics and run for office.

Bush graduated from Phillips Academy in 1964. In the fall he planned to once again follow in his father's footsteps and enter Yale. But first he returned to Texas to help the elder Bush run for a seat in the U.S. Senate. A member of the Republican Party, George H. W. Bush was challenging a Democratic incumbent. At the time, Democrats dominated politics in Texas and across most of the South.

George W., who had sometimes traveled with his father during the campaign, spent Election Day with his family. The elder Bush lost badly, and some friends later saw George W. crying.

While at Phillips Academy, Bush was a cheerleader as well as an athlete.

But back at Yale, he was once again his fun-loving, energetic self. And two years later the family celebrated when George H. W. Bush won a seat in the U.S. House of Representatives. For most of the next three decades, George W. would see his father's fame and political influence grow.

At Yale the younger Bush continued the patterns seen at Phillips Academy. He was an average student, but he made friends easily and enjoyed sports. He joined a fraternity and was elected its president. A friend from those days later said Bush was "a natural leader and a good guy to be with." He would remain close to many of the friends he made, and they would later help when he launched his political career.

Although Bush enjoyed an active social life, he found he didn't share the same views as some Yale students. The 1960s was a decade filled with conflict, both in the United States and around the world. Many young Americans, the baby boomers, protested against war in Vietnam, injustice, and old values. Bush, however, was more **conservative** and did not see a need for great change. He tended to accept his father's political views on Vietnam and other issues. The elder Bush supported the U.S. troops, who had been charged with helping South Vietnam fight local rebels and soldiers from neighboring North Vietnam.

An Era of Protest

The 1960s saw several massive rallies and protests against social conditions and government policies. The first protests targeted the unfair treatment of African Americans, especially in the South. By the start of the decade, the Reverend Martin Luther King Jr. was the leader of the civil rights movement, which fought for equal treatment of blacks. In 1963 Dr. King spoke in front of 250,000 people in Washington, D.C. The "I have a dream" speech he gave that day is one of the most famous in U.S. history. Several years later, the first of many protests against the Vietnam War began. While George W. Bush was at Yale, students there held small protests against the war. A larger one was held at New York City's Columbia University in 1968. Bush and his friends were not among the young Americans protesting or demanding civil rights: "I just don't remember much protest. . . . But maybe I just missed it. I wasn't looking for it. I wasn't much of a protester."

Piloting and Politics

During the war, many young men did not want to be drafted into the military and sent to Vietnam. During the times of heaviest fighting, hundreds of American soldiers were dying every week. Men could avoid being drafted, however, if they attended college. Some young men also joined the National Guard, rather than wait to be drafted. Unlike today, during the 1960s National Guard units rarely went to fight in foreign wars.

Shortly before graduating from Yale in 1968, Bush applied to join the Texas Air National Guard. He wanted to be a pilot, as his father had been during World War II. Years later, when he first ran for president, some people wondered whether George W. Bush had joined the National Guard to avoid the draft. He denied the charge, stating that if his unit had been sent to Vietnam, "I was prepared to go."

During the late 1960s, Bush's interest in politics continued to grow. As he spent the next two years learning to fly military jets, he also worked on political campaigns. In the fall of 1968, while in Florida, he helped a Republican running for the U.S. Senate. Two years later, his father ran for the Senate, and Bush sometimes spoke to the media to offer his father's views. In 1972 Bush helped run a campaign for an Alabama Republican.

In 1968 Bush joined the Texas Air National Guard. Here he is seen in the cockpit of an F-102.

Bush had returned to Texas in 1970, still flying for the Guard on weekends. Over the next few years, he took several jobs, including one helping poor children in Houston. His father also held different jobs. In 1971 he was named the U.S. ambassador to the **United Nations**. Two years later, the elder Bush became the head of the Republican National Committee, which helps the party's candidates run for election. George W., though, was unsure of what to do next. He later said, "There are some people who, the minute they get out of college, know exactly what they want to do. I did not. And it didn't bother me. That's just the way it was."

Bush finally decided to go to graduate school, and in 1973 he entered Harvard University to obtain a master's degree in business administration. Classmates and teachers saw in him a natural talent for leadership. One professor later said, "He was very good at getting along with people and getting things done."

Bush earned his master's degree in 1975 and was ready to enter business. But politics was often still on his mind.

Making a Name for Himself

$\mathcal{G}$eorge W. Bush never felt totally comfortable at Harvard or Yale. Despite his family's roots on the East Coast, he was a Texan, and he was determined to succeed in his adopted state. He returned to Midland, still a booming center for the U.S. oil industry. Taking money left over from an education fund, he went into business for himself as a landman. The work consisted of searching land records and maps, looking for land that might have oil or other resources beneath it. Then he would ask the owner to sell the land or the right to drill on it. In 1977 Bush named his company Arbusto—Spanish for "bush."

That summer Bush met Laura Welch, a librarian. They dated for three months, then married. Bush now had a new wife, a new house, and a new company. But he wanted something else—a political career. Just before meeting Laura, he had decided to run for Congress, even though he had never run for office before.

Political Lessons

To begin his career in politics, Bush would have to win the Republican Party nomination for a seat in Congress so he could face the Democratic candidate in the fall of 1974. Bush presented conservative views, complaining about a "federal government that is encroaching [interfering] more and more on our lives." In general, conservatives want small, less powerful governments so people

The Future First Lady

Laura Welch's love of books led to her career in education, as both a teacher and a school librarian. She and George W. Bush both grew up in Midland and had attended the same middle school. For a time, they also lived in the same apartment building in Houston. Although she did not know George W. well, she knew about his famous father. At first, she didn't think she had much in common with the younger Bush. But the two quickly learned that they did share many friends and interests.

Laura later said, "In a lot of ways I guess I felt like I'd known him all my life without really having known him that well." Later, she worked on his presidential campaigns, helping to get him elected. As First Lady, she started a new program to help young children learn to read and began the National Book Festival. Laura and George W. Bush have two children, twin daughters Jenna and Barbara.

have the freedom to live as they choose. Especially important was the freedom to make money, and Bush voiced his support for "free enterprise, the philosophy of growth."

In his campaign, Bush had several advantages. He knew wealthy people who would give him money. And his father was one of the most important Texan in national politics. The elder Bush had announced he would seek the Republican nomination for president in 1980.

George W. won his battle for the Republican nomination in Texas, but he faced a difficult race for the congressional seat. Bush's opponent stressed the Bush family's roots in Connecticut, suggesting that the young candidate was not truly a Texan. His family's wealth and social ties made them different from the average residents of the region. At one point, Bush met with voters on a farm and said, "Today is the first time I've been on a real farm." The comment suggested how different his life was from the experiences of many local residents. In the end, George W. Bush lost his election.

But the loss was helpful in some ways. Bush made friends and impressed people with his energy. He enjoyed meeting and talking with voters, and they seemed to like him, too. And Bush learned that he could not let political opponents suggest he was not a true Texan or a true conservative. He would build his career in Texas and make sure everyone knew where he stood on key issues.

PERSONAL STRUGGLES

For the next several years Bush worked on building up his company. An uncle helped him find investors, and the company drilled oil wells across West Texas. About half of them did not produce

eorge Bush for Congress

ON NOVEMBER 7,
VOTE FOR WEST TEXAS.
VOTE FOR
George Bush for Congress

Dear Voters,
   Laura and I would like
thank you for the many ki
during my campaign for th
   You've listened to me, ar
think. And hundreds of y
my campaign.
   I am very grateful to all o
   During the past twelve m
much I want to represen
mean that. I know I can do
   Again, our thanks.

oil, and many of the investors lost money. "I'm not going to pretend it was any huge success at the time," he later said. But he and his employees, he added, "developed a reputation as honest operators who worked hard, who gave people a fair shake."

In 1984 Bush merged his company with another oil company, Spectrum 7. He became a part owner of Spectrum 7 and served as its leader. The new company faced tough times in 1986, when the price of oil fell sharply. Spectrum 7 merged with another company, and Bush left the oil business for good.

That same year Bush made important changes in his personal life. He had long enjoyed drinking beer with his friends, though sometimes he drank too much. Years before, he had almost gotten into a fight with his father after a night of drinking. And in 1976 he had been arrested in Maine for drinking and driving. After his fortieth birthday, Bush gave up drinking completely.

The year before, he had begun to think about his relationship with God. Bush had attended different Christian churches, but never had a deep faith. Finally, as he later wrote, he began to "recommit my heart to Jesus Christ." That included reading the Bible often, at times daily. Bush was now a "born-again," or **fundamentalist**, Christian, and his relationship with other conservative Christians would play a strong role in his life.

Political Victories

By 1980 Bush had seen his father seek the Republican presidential nomination and lose, only to be named the party's vice presidential candidate, which made him part of Ronald Reagan's winning ticket. The elder Bush served with Reagan, one of the more popular presidents of the twentieth century. The two Reagan-Bush terms saw the United States improve relations with its major international rival, the Soviet Union. The U.S. economy also grew for much of Reagan's presidency.

While vice president, George H. W. Bush continued to think about becoming president himself and planned to run in 1988. Early in 1987, George W. went to Washington to help with his father's campaign. He became, as one Bush family friend said, Vice President Bush's "eyes and ears," since the elder Bush "knew he could rely on W. to report truthfully on what was going on."

THE REAGAN "REVOLUTION"

With the election of Ronald Reagan, conservatives and fundamentalist Christians began to play a larger role in U.S. politics. Reagan appealed to Americans who had disliked the protests and social changes of the 1960s and early 1970s. He promised to restore Americans' pride after those difficult years. Reagan defeated President Jimmy Carter, who had been in office when the U.S. economy struggled. Carter also failed in his attempt to rescue Americans kidnapped in Iran at the end of 1979. Years later, after George W. Bush had won the presidency in 2000, some political observers suggested that he and Reagan shared some personal traits. Both made friends easily and put people at ease. Both disliked being bothered with details about issues. In politics, the two presidents pushed for tax cuts and a strong military. Unlike Reagan, however, Bush did not often reach out to Democrats to solve problems. And unlike Reagan, Bush left the White House with a low approval rating.

George W. (center) accompanied his father, who was campaigning for the presidency in 1988.

When the election finally came, Vice President Bush won easily, and George W. now had the U.S. president as his father. But the younger Bush did not want to stay in Washington, D.C. He helped his father choose some of the members of his cabinet, then returned to Texas before the end of the year.

NEW CHALLENGES FOR FATHER AND SON

Even before going back to Texas, Bush was thinking about his own political future. He considered running for governor of Texas, but he knew he had to prove to the voters that he was not just the president's son. He agreed with Roland Betts, an old friend from Yale, who told him, "You need to do something on your own, need to get your own name out there and develop your own reputation."

A group of Texas investors asked Bush to become a part owner of the Texas Rangers, a Major League Baseball team. Bush didn't have a lot of money to invest, but his future partners liked the idea of working with the son of the president. They also knew that Bush had a genuine love of baseball. The deal was completed in April 1989, and Bush soon became one of the two managing partners of the team. He was the owner the public saw at the games, joking with players and fans. He spoke Spanish with the Hispanic players, and at times would call out, "Hey Bat[boy], you got some bubble gum?" When he received the gum, Bush gave it out to the fans. Bush had a clear talent for getting along with all sorts of people.

While Bush enjoyed himself at the ballpark, his father faced the difficulties of being president of the United States. The elder Bush's biggest challenge came in August 1990 when President Saddam Hussein of Iraq launched an invasion of neighboring Kuwait. The United States had supported Saddam during most of the 1980s when his country fought a long war against Iran. The support continued even after Saddam used deadly chemical weapons to kill Iranians and some of his own people. But Kuwait was a U.S. ally, as it supplied oil to the Americans. President Bush began to assemble a **coalition** of dozens of nations to drive out the Iraqis.

The Gulf War against Saddam and his forces began in January 1991. With U.S. troops leading the way, coalition troops quickly drove the Iraqis out of Kuwait. Some Americans called for the U.S. military to advance to the Iraqi capital of Baghdad and remove Saddam from power. President Bush said no, since the United Nations had not given the coalition permission to do so. But U.S., British, and French war planes began flying over large parts of the country, to prevent Saddam from threatening Iraqis who opposed his tyrannical rule.

The End of the Cold War

The struggle between the United States and the Soviet Union called the cold war began after World War II. Each nation tried to win allies and weaken the other's influence around the world. During George H. W. Bush's presidency, the cold war, which Reagan had carried on relentlessly, finally ended. The Soviet Union could no longer afford to spend heavily on its military, while the United States could. And Soviet citizens were tired of their political system, communism, which limited their freedoms. The collapse of the Soviet Union in 1991 made the United States the world's only superpower—a nation with great military might. Some conservative American politicians thought the end of the cold war gave the United States a greater chance to shape events around the world. Their goal was to spread democracy and protect U.S. interests. A few of these conservatives became advisers to George W. Bush and shaped his policies during the wars that followed the terrorist attacks of September 11, 2001.

A Bitter Defeat

Across the United States Americans applauded the easy victory over Iraq. But even before the Gulf War, the U.S. economy had begun to sour. Following the Gulf War, in a pronounced downturn called a recession, several million people lost their jobs and the value of homes fell. The recession officially ended in 1991, but the economy did not regain strength right away. To some degree, voters blamed President Bush, and the issue haunted him when he ran for reelection as president in 1992.

George H. W. Bush faced two opponents in his second run for the presidency—Democrat Bill Clinton and a fellow Texan, H. Ross Perot, who had formed his own party. Perot drew support from some independents and Republicans who might otherwise have voted for Bush. That helped Bill Clinton win the election, a bitter defeat for the whole Bush family. George W. later said the loss brought out "strong emotions in me, to see a good man get whipped."

But the loss was a plus for George W.'s own career. He had considered running for governor of Texas in 1990. He chose not to, partly because he lacked experience, and partly because his mother, Barbara Bush, did not think he should run while his father was president. Now George W. had become better known across Texas because of his time with the Rangers. He'd been successful at something without his family's help. And with his father out of the White House, he could take the next major step in his political career—running for governor of Texas.

GOVERNOR BUSH

*W*orking on his father's campaigns, Bush had learned a valuable lesson: loyalty is important in politics. He wanted aides and advisers who put serving his interests over their own needs. He already had one trusted aide—Karl Rove. Others, such as Karen Hughes, would soon join him. But more importantly, he needed the support of his wife, Laura. As Bush later said, "She wanted to make sure this was something I really wanted to do." He assured her he wanted to run so he could make Texas a better state.

As he began his campaign, Bush stressed several issues. The top one was education. He thought the state should not only give towns more money for schools but also allow them more control over running the schools. He was also concerned about welfare, the government system that assists some poor people with money

George W. Bush campaigns for governor of Texas. His campaign covered key issues such as education and welfare.

and other forms of support. He wanted people on welfare to go to school or train for a job. He said, "Dependency [relying] on government saps the soul and drains the spirit of our very future."

The campaign had some difficult moments. Some reporters suggested that the Bush family had used its influence to get the candidate into the National Guard back in 1968. They also raised the question of whether he had chosen the Guard to avoid serving in Vietnam. Bush denied having received special treatment and pointed out that he took risks flying military jets, even in the United States. "Had that engine failed, I could have been killed."

Running a State

In the end, Bush easily won the election. His supporters included some conservative Democrats who had once supported Ronald Reagan. Democrats also controlled the Texas legislature, which makes the state's laws. Bush had to work closely with the party's top lawmakers to fulfill most of his campaign promises.

Bush took his job seriously, starting his workday each morning before 8:00 o'clock. He expected his aides to be prepared, and he liked short meetings. Under the Texas constitution, the governor does not have a

George W. Bush takes the oath of office in January 1994 as wife Laura looks on.

lot of power. Someone once told Bush that the governor's office was weak in comparison to other parts of the government. Bush said, "Only for a weak person." Bush saw himself as strong and able to get things done.

Education remained his top issue. At the time he took office, the state was already taking steps to improve education. Bush promoted reading programs for younger children and pushed for students to score higher on statewide tests. Many black and Hispanic students showed gains on these tests while Bush was governor. But critics pointed out that Texas started as one of the worst states in the nation on public education. During and after Bush's term as governor, its schools remained weak in comparison to those in most other states.

THE OTHER GOVERNOR BUSH

George W. Bush was not the only member of the family running for office in 1994. His younger brother Jeb was hoping to become governor of Florida. The Bush family and their friends had considered Jeb the most likely of the children to run for an important political office. He was more serious than the fun-loving George W. and a better student. Jeb moved to Florida in 1981, going into the real estate business with one of his father's friends. Unlike his older brother, Jeb was better at business and soon became a millionaire. He was named Florida's secretary of commerce in 1987. Jeb Bush lost his race for governor in 1994 but won when he ran again in 1998 and 2002. In 2000 his state played a key role in the election that put his brother in the White House.

George W. Bush reads to elementary school children in Round Rock, Texas. Education was a top issue for him as governor of the state.

During the 1990s many Americans grew increasingly concerned about the environment. They sought cleaner water and air and less use of fuels thought to add to global warming. Bush had not made the environment one of his key issues, but he promised Texans, "First and foremost, we are committed to clean air in the state of Texas." Yet during the Bush years, the federal government said Texas had the worst air pollution in the nation. Bush, as a conservative, wanted the government to play a less active role in people's lives. He wanted companies to volunteer to reduce their pollution, rather than having the state force them. The critics called this voluntary plan a failure.

Bush also showed his conservative values when it came to helping the poor. He believed religious groups should play a large role, using funds from the government in addition to contributions from their own members. He promoted laws that let "faith-based" charities do more to help people in need. "What government cannot do is get people to love one another," he once said. "You can't pass a law that does that. That comes from a higher authority [God]." Bush later used the term "compassionate conservatism" to describe his approach to helping the needy. He wanted to help others, but he wanted to reduce the government's role in the process.

NATIONAL ATTENTION

In 1997, while still in his first term as governor, George W. Bush knew some Republicans were already considering him as a presidential candidate in 2000. Party leaders knew about his mostly successful term as governor. Most average voters around the country, however, knew only his famous name. Then, a legal issue in Texas made international news, and Bush was at the center of it.

Karla Faye Tucker, found guilty of murder in 1984, had been sentenced to die. While awaiting execution in a Texas prison, Tucker became a fundamentalist Christian and expressed great remorse for what she had done at a time when she was addicted to drugs. She and many people who believed she was now sorry for her crime asked Bush to prevent her execution, scheduled for February 3, 1998. Tucker's supporters included at least one well-known Republican lawmaker and a famous TV minister.

The case drew attention because of Tucker's new faith and because she was a woman. Texas had not executed a woman in more than a century, and few other states had in recent years. Bush, however, denied the appeals for mercy. As he later wrote, he supported the death penalty because, "if administered swiftly and justly, capital punishment is a deterrent against future violence and will save other innocent lives." Bush said he had to follow the laws of the state. Tucker had received a fair trial and admitted her guilt. A board that reviews pleas for **pardons** had rejected Tucker's claim. After her death, Bush said, "I had done the right thing in upholding the laws of Texas."

THE OTHER DEATH SENTENCE

Henry Lee Lucas was another notorious Texas murderer facing execution in 1998. He claimed he had lied when he had confessed to the murder that led to his death sentence. Evidence seemed to back up his story. Investigators learned that he had been nowhere near Texas the night of the murder he had said he'd committed. Still, he had committed other crimes in the state. Governor Bush decided to change his sentence to life in prison. "There is no chance he will ever walk free," Bush told reporters. "He's a very bad man." Some papers suggested that Bush had taken a risk by preventing Lucas's execution. Many Texans favored the death penalty. But Bush decided that Lucas could not be killed for a murder he did not commit.

Reelection and Beyond

Bush tried to stay focused on his reelection, rather than thinking ahead to 2000. But soon after winning in November, his aides were gathering information for him on key national issues. And early in 1999 he began traveling the country, raising millions of dollars for his presidential campaign.

By that time Bush was a millionaire himself. He had sold his share of the Texas Rangers in 1998, and that investment had yielded more than $12 million in profit. But he wouldn't use his own money to run for president. Few candidates for any office can afford to pay for their own campaigns, especially to run television ads. Presidential campaigns are the most expensive, since candidates must travel across the country, run ads in many states, and campaign for a year or more. Those candidates count on many supporters to give money, especially wealthy Americans. Once again, Bush turned to friends and business contacts for some of the money he needed. By the end of June 1999, he had collected more than $36 million.

Becoming a National Candidate

Bush joined a crowded field of Republicans seeking to win their party's nomination. Nine other people entered the race, though some dropped out before the primaries and caucuses. These elections are held in the states at different times before a presidential election, so Republican and Democratic voters can choose their party's candidates. As 1999 went on, Bush's main opponents were Steve Forbes, a wealthy publisher, and Senator John McCain of Arizona. Bush, though, was favored by most Republicans, according to national polls.

Republican presidential candidate George W. Bush waves to the crowd at a rally in Kentucky prior to the Republican National Convention.

Bush set out several major issues he wanted to tackle as president. Improving education and cutting taxes were at the top of the list. He also promised, once again, to be a compassionate conservative. Bush said America had gone "from accepting responsibility to assigning blame. As governments did more and more, people were required to do less and less." Bush said the government could not and should not solve all problems. "That does not mean we should not help people. It means we should look for more effective means of help." Churches, charities, and local governments could provide some of that help. But people had to do some things for themselves. And they had to accept responsibility for their actions, which meant paying a price if they did something wrong.

Through the summer and fall of 1999, Bush traveled the country, spreading his message. The national media began to pay close attention to his speeches, and many observers noticed that the candidate sometimes misspoke. Bush used the wrong words or said things that didn't seem to make sense. He once said he knew it was hard to "put food on your family" and said "admissions" instead of "emissions" when referring to automotive exhaust. Bush was not comfortable when people asked questions he wasn't ready for. Some of his problems in public led some reporters to think he wasn't smart—or at least not smart enough

DIRTY TRICKS?

In South Carolina some people said the Bush campaign used "dirty tricks" to defeat John McCain. In politics, these tricks include such things as spreading lies about opponents or tying up their phone lines with crank calls. In South Carolina Bush appeared with a local McCain opponent who said the senator had never helped America's former soldiers. McCain had been a war hero and been held as a prisoner during the Vietnam War. He knew how veterans suffered and took pride in trying to help them. Other veterans disputed the charge against McCain and asked Bush to condemn the statement. Bush refused. By not saying anything, Bush seemed to suggest that he agreed the charge was true.

Early in the race for the presidential nomination, Senator John McCain (right) beat Bush in the February 2000 New Hampshire primary.

to be president. But in small groups he spoke easily and had a better command of facts on key issues.

In November 1999 Bush's aides began to worry for the first time. Senator McCain had moved past him in one poll. In February 2000 the two men faced each other in the New Hampshire primary, the first in the nation. McCain stunned Bush by winning easily. Bush realized he would have to work harder to win the nomination.

That loss was followed by many wins in other important states. By May Bush was clearly going to be the Republican candidate for president. Vice President Al Gore was on his way to winning the Democratic nomination. Gore, like Bush, came from a family with deep roots in politics. The two men would face off in one of the closest elections in U.S. history.

THE "UNITER" TAKES CHARGE

*I*n late July 2000 thousands of Republicans gathered in Philadelphia for their party's national convention. They met to
officially name George W. Bush as the Republican candidate
for president. He then announced his choice for the vice presidential candidate: Dick Cheney.

*In July 2000, George W. Bush was named the Republican candidate for president. He chose Dick
Cheney (right) as his vice president.*

Changing Role of Conventions

U.S. political parties held their first conventions during the 1830s. Party leaders made speeches promoting the candidates of their choice. The people representing the different states, the convention delegates, then proceeded to select the party's nominee. At times, the party leaders made deals with one another away from the convention floor, giving or taking away support for a candidate. The delegates generally voted the way their state leaders told them to. At some conventions, the delegates have had to vote many times to choose a candidate. By the time George W. Bush was nominated in 2000, however, the suspense had been eliminated. This is because the primaries gave the voters in the states the power to choose the delegates for the convention, and it was understood that each delegate would vote for the candidate favored by the voters in his or her state. Bush knew months before the Philadelphia convention that he had enough delegates to win.

Cheney had held many government positions. Perhaps most important, he had been secretary of defense during the presidency of George H. W. Bush. The Bushes trusted him to do what was best for George W. As Bush said, "I'm going to need somebody who's seen things before, who can give me advice to make good decisions."

At the convention, Bush could not attack the Clinton/Gore record on the economy. It had been strong during the Clinton years, though the country would soon enter a recession. But he suggested that the Democrats had let the military grow weak and had not made the country better. "So much promise," Bush told the convention, "to no great purpose." Gore, Bush said, would just continue the policies of President Clinton, but Bush wanted to cut the ties to the past: "It is a time for new beginnings."

The Final Push for the Presidency

The Democrats held their convention a few weeks later. Gore was a **liberal**. He opposed the tax cuts Bush said he would seek as president. Gore said that the cuts favored the rich and that Republicans too often supported the interests of the wealthy and big businesses. "They're for the powerful, and we're for the people." Gore said he would strengthen programs that helped the elderly, such as Medicare and Social Security. He also promised to protect the civil rights of all minorities.

With the conventions over, the two presidential candidates and their families crisscrossed the country, looking for votes. They met in three debates shown on television. Bush asserted that his time as governor gave him the experience he needed to run the country. He stressed that he was able to work with Democrats in Texas and would encourage the same cooperation in Washington, as well. "It will require the ability of a Republican president to reach out . . . and to say to Democrats, let's come together to do what is right for America. It's been my record as Governor of Texas, it will be how I conduct myself if I'm fortunate enough to earn your vote."

On foreign policy, Bush said he would not try to build democracy in nations that did not have it. The U.S. military, if it had to fight foreign wars, should leave as soon as possible

Al Gore (left) and George W. Bush debate at the University of Massachusetts–Boston, in October 2000. This was the first of three debates between the two candidates.

afterward. The people within a nation, Bush said, had to create their governments for themselves.

During the campaign, Bush faced questions about his past. Some people suggested that Bush had used illegal drugs. He refused to answer the question directly, though earlier he had said he never used drugs after 1974. Then, a few days before the election, the media reported that in 1976 he had been arrested for drinking and driving. The news did not seem to hurt his campaign. Top aide Karl Rove was predicting an easy Republican victory.

On election night, however, the Bushes watched with concern as the results came in. A candidate needs 270 electoral votes to become president. Each state casts as many votes in the electoral college as the number of lawmakers it has in Congress. In general, the candidate who wins the most votes cast by a state's citizens wins the state's electoral votes. Candidates focus on winning the electoral votes of the states with the largest populations. Bush had counted on winning Florida, where his brother Jeb was governor.

Sitting in an Austin, Texas, restaurant, Bush heard that one television network was predicting that Gore would win Florida. The vice president was also winning in several other large states. Bush and his family left the restaurant and returned to the governor's mansion. For several hours, they watched the election results pour in. As the night went on, the television network took back its claim that Gore had won Florida. Late at night, while Bush was in bed, the reports said he would win Florida, which would give him 271 electoral votes—just enough to win. But by the next morning, November 8, no one knew who had won Florida. The vote was too close to call.

A BITTER BATTLE

The result in Florida was to determine the next president. Gore had won more popular votes across the country, but he, like Bush, needed Florida's electoral votes to win the election. Bush seemed to have the lead in the state's votes, but Gore's aides suggested that there had been problems with some of the electronic **ballots**. On November 9, Gore filed a lawsuit demanding that the votes be recounted by hand in several Florida counties.

As the political race moved to the courts, Bush and his legal team sued to stop the recount. They supported the actions of Katherine Harris, Florida's secretary of state. One of her jobs

ELECTION 2000

12 PAGES OF COVERAGE INSIDE

The Miami Herald

WEDNESDAY, NOVEMBER 8, 2000 ▸ FINAL EDITION

www.herald.com

35 Cents
For home delivery, call 305 350-2000

BUSH WINS IT

FLORIDA PROVIDES THE CRUCIAL MARGIN

FATEFUL WAIT: Texas Gov. George W. Bush waves to supporters in Bentonville, Ark., while making his last campaign stop.

PAUL J. RICHARDS/AFP

ON HOME TURF: Vice President Al Gore steps out of the voting booth near his home in Elmwood, Tenn., after casting his personal ballot.

J. SCOTT APPLEWHITE/AP

Republicans keep control of Congress

Though the Republican presidential victory was contested by the Democratic Party, The Miami Herald *claimed the victory for George W. Bush on November 8, 2000.*

was to oversee elections and report official results. She planned to approve the results that showed Bush winning, even if recounts were still going on. Harris angered the Democrats, because she, a staunch Republican, had clearly favored Bush in the election, helping run his campaign in Florida. The Florida courts ruled that Harris had to let the recounts continue before releasing an official result. Bush then challenged this

ELECTION WOES

The 2000 presidential election introduced Americans to new terms along with great controversy. Political experts talked about "hanging chads"—the little pieces of paper that can cling to a ballot if the voting machines are not well maintained. And a kind of ballot called the "butterfly" seemed to cause confusion. It had a single row of holes for voters to punch, with the candidates' names listed on either side. Gore made two arguments: that the voting machines improperly rejected some votes intended for him because of the hanging chads, and that the butterfly ballots were so confusing that thousands of people who'd intended to vote for Gore had mistakenly voted for Bush. The "hanging chad" ballots were not counted, although the actual pieces of paper were retained and later inspected. The Democrats said many of those ballots were from people who wanted to vote for Gore. One study after the election seemed to show Gore was right. If all the votes that were meant for Gore had been counted, he would have won. The Republicans argued there was no real proof of this. Another study gave Bush more votes than the official count, but he still beat Gore by fewer than 1,500 votes.

decision in the U.S. Supreme Court. For the first time in U.S. history, the country's top court was asked to help decide a presidential election.

Meanwhile, back in Texas, Bush tried to stay busy on his ranch near Crawford, a little town in the west central part of the state. At times, he met with advisers. He had to prepare for taking over the presidency if the Court ruled in his favor. He rarely met with reporters, and when he did, he didn't say much about the legal battle. One friend told a reporter, "More than anything, he's uncomfortable. He doesn't like a mess."

On December 12, the "mess" finally ended. In a 5–4 vote, the Supreme Court ruled that the recounts should stop. Katherine Harris could announce the results she had, which showed Bush winning Florida by 537 votes. The next day, Al Gore conceded defeat, and Bush spoke to the nation. The close election and the battle over the results showed that Americans were deeply divided. Bush said, "Together, guided by a spirit of common sense, common courtesy and common goals, we can unite and inspire the American citizens." This idea was linked to something from his campaign, when he had said he was a "uniter, not a divider." Starting on January 20, 2001, the day he officially became the forty-third U.S. president, Bush would have a chance to prove that to the nation. Many Democrats, however, thought a conservative Supreme Court had given Bush a victory he had not earned.

THE NEW PRESIDENT

At his inauguration, Bush outlined what he hoped to accomplish as president. He wanted to show that he was a uniter: "This is my solemn pledge: I will work to build a single nation of justice

A Diverse Cabinet

Every president has a cabinet, consisting of the heads of government agencies that also serve as presidential advisers. Presidents often seek a range of political views in their cabinets. They also choose people from different parts of the country and representatives of different ethnic or racial groups. George W. Bush made history when he chose Colin Powell as the country's first African American secretary of state. Powell, an army general, had served as the top military adviser to President George H. W. Bush. As secretary of state, he would help shape the younger Bush's foreign policy. Powell would also bring his expertise on military affairs. Bush also named the first Asian American to serve as secretary of labor, Elaine Chao. And during his second term, he named as attorney general Alberto Gonzalez, the first Hispanic to occupy that position.

and opportunity." Throughout the speech, he made reference to God, the Bible, and America's history. Even some liberals admitted it was a fine speech. One Democrat wrote, "It was by far the best inaugural address in 40 years."

As promised, Bush dove into his top two issues: tax cuts and education. The country was entering a recession, and Bush argued that cutting taxes would give people and businesses more money to invest. At the time the country also had a large budget surplus. During most of the Clinton years the government had taken in more money than it spent. In February 2001 Bush told the nation that his tax cut "is needed. It is necessary. It will make a very positive difference in the lives of people who pay taxes, and our country can afford it." Soon Congress passed a bill that cut taxes by $1.3 trillion over ten years.

For education, Bush worked closely with Democratic senator Edward Kennedy of Massachusetts to create the No Child Left Behind Act. The law emphasized the need for higher test scores as proof that students were learning more in school. If students in poorly performing schools did not improve their scores the schools had to provide extra help. States and towns also had more freedom to spend money from the federal government as they chose. The new law also promised more federal money for education.

The president also talked about the environment. His first actions upset people seeking to defend the environment, as he called for drilling for oil in Alaska's Arctic National Wildlife Refuge. He also said the government would stop placing environmental restrictions on manufacturing companies, making it easier for them to operate. This started a pattern, as throughout his presidency Bush tried to make it easier for businesses to develop

Bush waves during a bill signing ceremony for the No Child Left Behind Act in Hamilton, Ohio.

natural resources in protected areas or to avoid limits on pollution. One environmental group accused Bush of committing hundreds of "crimes against nature."

Looking Overseas

In foreign affairs, the United States had several concerns. It wanted good relations with Russia, the powerful country created following the collapse of the Soviet Union at the end of the cold war. U.S. officials were also concerned about China. It was an important trading partner, but also a growing military power. Tensions rose a bit in April, after a U.S spy plane collided with a Chinese military jet. The Chinese held the crew for eleven days. Another Asian country, North Korea, also took Bush's attention. The country was hostile to the United States and was found to be working secretly to develop nuclear weapons, the deadliest weapons on Earth.

Perhaps Bush's top concern was Iraq and the Middle East. For decades, the United States was the major ally of Israel. The Jewish state faced constant threats from the region's Arab nations. In addition, Saddam Hussein was still in power in Iraq, and U.S. and British planes were still patrolling the skies over part of the country. At times, the Iraqis fired at the planes. In February Bush ordered bombing raids on Iraqi military positions near Baghdad. Later, he told reporters he was determined to stop Iraq from developing weapons of mass destruction, which could kill thousands of people at one time.

During the Clinton years, some Americans had called for removing Saddam from power, and the Democratic president had signed a bill, the Iraq Liberation Act, that made regime change in that country a U.S. goal. Clinton did not actively pursue this goal, however. Neither did Bush at first, though his aides discussed it. Events over the coming months would lead to new attention on Saddam and Iraq.

The Terrorist Threat

The Clinton years had seen a rise in terrorist attacks against the United States and its allies. By 1998 Clinton knew that Osama bin Laden was responsible for most of them. The president ordered a missile attack on a remote camp in Afghanistan, where bin Laden was thought to be living.

Osama bin Laden, leader of the Al Qaeda terrorist group, was responsible for many of the terrorist attacks against the United States prior to the presidency of George W. Bush.

TERROR THREAT TIMELINE

1993   Truck bomb kills six people and injures over a thousand in the garage of the World Trade Center in New York City

1995   Filipino police stop a plot to blow up a dozen U.S. airplanes in midair

1996   Truck bomb kills nineteen U.S. soldiers stationed in Saudi Arabia

1998   Attacks on U.S. embassies in Tanzania and Kenya kill 224 people

1999   U.S. officials catch a terrorist smuggling explosives into the country for a planned attack on Los Angeles International Airport

2000   A small boat filled with explosives almost sinks the U.S. warship *Cole* off the coast of Yemen

The terrorist leader escaped the attack. But he remained protected by Afghanistan's rulers, a group called the Taliban.

Bin Laden and the Taliban were conservative followers of **Islam**, the religion of the Muslims. Bin Laden had first come to Afghanistan during the 1980s. He belonged to a rich family from Saudi Arabia. Bin Laden helped the Afghanis as they fought Soviet troops, who had invaded Afghanistan in 1979. After the

Soviets pulled out in 1989, the country erupted into a long civil war. The Taliban came to power during the mid–1990s. They ended the violence but severely limited the people's freedoms. The Taliban ordered men to grow their beards, forbade dancing and the playing of music, and took away the legal rights of women. The Taliban also let bin Laden build camps to train as terrorists members of his organization, Al Qaeda—"the Base." Bin Laden believed that the United States too closely supported Israel and denied the rights of Arabs living under Israeli control. He also wanted the United States to pull all its military forces out of Saudi Arabia, the birthplace of Islam.

President Clinton left office believing that bin Laden and Al Qaeda posed a serious threat to the United States. He and his aides explained the danger to Bush and his advisers. During the spring and summer of 2001, U.S. intelligence agencies sensed that bin Laden might be planning a new attack. George Tenet was the head of the Central Intelligence Agency (CIA) at the time. He later said that the presumed attack could be "something very, very, very big. The system was blinking red."

In August, Bush and his advisers received a warning about the possible danger. Bush knew that bin Laden had talked about striking in the United States. But the new intelligence reports suggested that the next attack might happen overseas. Intelligence agents did not see the connection between the new warning and information they had about terrorists in the United States.

Then September 11 came. George W. Bush was about to receive a plan to give the CIA permission to arm remote-controlled planes. Their mission—track down bin Laden and kill him. But bin Laden struck first. And Americans realized that this time, the terrorist threat was not overseas.

For hours on September 11, Americans sat in front of their televisions watching the horrible images coming out of New York City. They saw one plane hit the World Trade Center, then another. They saw the buildings crumple, and thousands of people running through the city streets. President Bush, meanwhile, was flying to different military bases around the country. The Secret Service, which protects all U.S. presidents and their families, didn't want Bush to return to Washington, D.C., until they were sure he would be safe. By early evening, Bush was back in the nation's capital.

The next day Bush met with his top defense and intelligence advisers. The evidence seemed clear: Al Qaeda had carried out the hijackings. The CIA already had agents in Afghanistan working with groups that

One of the World Trade Center towers burns after being hit by a hijacked passenger plane on September 11, 2001.

opposed the harsh rule of the Taliban. Bush ordered the agency to increase its funding and activity in the mountainous country. His goal was to catch bin Laden if the Taliban refused to turn him over.

Later, addressing the nation, the president said America was facing a different kind of enemy than it had in the past. "This enemy hides in shadows, and has no regard for human life. This is an enemy who preys on innocent and unsuspecting people, then runs for cover. . . . This is an enemy that tries to hide. But it won't be able to hide forever."

As his father had in 1991, President Bush sought international help in fighting an overseas war. Some of his earlier actions suggested that Bush would not always have strong relations with foreign nations. He had called for a missile defense system that the Russians opposed. Even with the cold war over, Russia still wanted influence in Europe and Asia. Russian leaders believed that the missile system was meant to limit their military responses to any future crisis. Bush also upset some foreign leaders when he said the United States would withdraw from the Kyoto Protocol, an international agreement designed to lessen global warming. Now Bush wanted to reach out to other countries to find bin Laden and battle the terrorist threat. After the attacks of September 11, most nations were willing to help. As Bush later said, the other countries were "either . . . with us, or . . . with the terrorists."

AFGHANISTAN INVASION
As the military prepared for war and the State Department lined up allies, Bush and others wanted to know whether Iraq had been

involved in the attack. Some people in the administration believed the United States would face a terrorist threat from Iraq in the future, even if the Middle Eastern nation had not taken part in the September 11 attacks. Thus a number of aides were already talking about war with Iraq. Bush, however, wanted to stay focused on Afghanistan—at least for now. He ordered plans to be made for a future military invasion of Iraq, if that became necessary.

As U.S. leaders expected, the Taliban refused to turn over Osama bin Laden and other Al Qaeda leaders. So, on October 7, U.S. and British planes began bombing terrorist camps in Afghanistan. Taliban military bases were also targeted. The U.S.–led coalition wanted to destroy the Taliban government in Afghanistan, to prevent that nation from ever again hosting terrorists. Removing the Taliban would also increase the chances of bringing democracy to the country.

Announcing the bombing, Bush stressed that America was not attacking Muslims or their religion. He did not want to create anti-American feelings in Muslim countries or in any way suggest that the United States opposed or disrespected Islam. Still, within America, some Arabs and Muslims—or even people assumed to be Arabs or Muslims—faced discrimination after September 11. Americans feared new terrorist attacks and sometimes did not distinguish between the terrorists, who held extreme Islamic views, and other Muslims.

Along with the bombing, CIA agents worked with anti-Taliban forces in Afghanistan. Within several weeks, U.S. troops arrived, but most battles pitted the Taliban against the segment of the Afghan population that had opposed the extremists' rule all along. Through November, the Taliban lost ground and support from different tribes. By December 9, it no longer ruled Afghanistan.

Later in the month, Hamid Karzai took control, with the support of the United Nations. At the same time, specially trained U.S. forces tracked bin Laden and his followers into the Tora Bora Mountains. They let Afghan forces do most of the fighting there, and bin Laden managed to escape into Pakistan. Other Al Qaeda and Taliban members fled there, too, or into the Tora Bora and other sparsely populated mountainous regions of Afghanistan.

The United States took the lead in trying to keep peace in Afghanistan after the fall of the Taliban. In March 2002, U.S. troops battled some of the terrorists still in the country. But already, the Bush administration was changing its focus on the war on terror. Iraq would be the next target.

The War on Terror at Home

The September 11 attacks united Americans around the president. Bush's popularity soared as Democrats and Republicans alike saw him take bold steps to challenge Al Qaeda and prevent new attacks. The president created a new agency, the Department of Homeland Security, to control the antiterrorist efforts. He also called for new laws that would make it easier to gather intelligence about terrorists. If lawmakers sometimes opposed parts of his plans, he wasn't afraid to challenge them. He told Republican leaders, "Why are you obstructing our efforts? This is a time to be supporting your president!"

Bush and his aides counted on loyalty from most Americans during this time of crisis. The president became less likely to listen to concerns from Democrats, or even members of his party. Bush was confident that he knew what to do. He had to lead the country through difficult times, in a battle of good versus evil. His critics, however, began to see him as arrogant. He seemed to

The PATRIOT Act

One of the laws President Bush sought was called the Uniting and Strengthening America by Providing Appropriate Tools Required to Intercept and Obstruct Terrorism Act. The name was shortened to the USA PATRIOT Act, or just the Patriot Act. The law upset Americans concerned about civil liberties, which include the rights to privacy and free speech. The act gave police new powers to secretly listen in on phone conversations or check a person's records at a public library. Opponents of the act feared the police could abuse their new powers and use them against innocent Americans. Democratic senator Russ Feingold of Wisconsin said the law violated the Constitution. But in the anger and worry after September 11, Feingold was one of only a few lawmakers who spoke against the Patriot Act.

follow his own plan no matter what facts were presented. And the critics disliked an attitude Bush seemed to display—if you disagreed with him or his administration, you were disloyal to the country. That concern grew as Bush made his case for war with Iraq.

A Growing Threat?

While the fighting was still raging in Afghanistan, President Bush challenged Saddam Hussein. The Iraqi leader had kicked out inspectors from the United Nations looking for weapons of mass destruction (WMDs). Bush feared Iraq might give those weapons to terrorists or use them on Iraq's enemies in the region, particularly Israel. Bush told Saddam to let the UN inspectors back into the country. A few months later, in January 2002, Bush gave his first State of the Union address. He said Iraq was part of an "axis of evil, aiming to threaten the peace of the world." Bush was moving closer to saying that the United States would invade Iraq if

The Bush administration viewed Iraqi leader Saddam Hussein as a threat to world peace.

Saddam seemed to present a threat to American security.

Over the next few months, Bush and his aides looked over intelligence about Iraq's WMD program. Vice President Dick Cheney and Secretary of Defense Donald Rumsfeld were among those who believed that Saddam was a true threat. In August Cheney said, "Simply stated, there is no doubt that Saddam Hussein now has weapons of mass destruction. There is no doubt he is amassing them to use against our friends, against our allies, and against us." Bush himself made similar comments. But within the White House and intelligence agencies, some people disagreed about the level of danger Saddam posed. The intelligence was not clear. Most of the data seemed to suggest that Iraq was not a threat at the moment. Cheney and others chose to believe the worst possible reports, even if the evidence was not solid. They also believed that even if Saddam let weapons inspectors return, he would be able to keep producing weapons of mass destruction.

In September Bush spoke at the United Nations in New York City. He said the United States wanted to work with the UN to end the threat Saddam posed. But the Americans were

THE BUSH DOCTRINE

In foreign affairs, several U.S. presidents have issued doctrines, or statements of how the country would act if foreign nations threatened U.S. interests. The first was the Monroe Doctrine of 1821. James Monroe, the fifth president, said that the United States would not accept European involvement in the political issues of North and South America. In 1980 President Jimmy Carter stated the Carter Doctrine: that the United States saw the Persian Gulf as vital to the country's interests and would not stand by if other nations threatened the region. After September 11, George W. Bush presented several new ideas that became part of the Bush Doctrine. One dealt with preventive wars. Although it's generally agreed that a country has the right to strike first when an enemy is obviously about to attack, Bush called for preventive wars "even if uncertainty remains as to the time and place of the enemy's attack." Critics said the doctrine might tempt the United States to attack before it had used diplomacy or the influence of the UN to prevent a war. The doctrine seemed to suggest that the United States could use its power whenever it feared a threat, whether the danger was real or not. The Bush Doctrine was used to support the war against Iraq.

ready to strike alone if Saddam refused UN demands. In October Congress gave Bush the power to carry out an attack on Iraq if he thought it necessary to "(1) defend the national security of the United States against the continuing threat posed by Iraq; and (2) enforce all relevant United Nations Security Council resolutions regarding Iraq."

Bush, though, once again wanted an international coalition. Over the next few months, he found more than thirty nations willing to help, including Great Britain, Australia, Spain, and Poland. The UN refused to give its permission for an invasion, but by March 2003 Bush was ready to attack. He issued a threat to Saddam, telling him to give up power or face a war. Saddam ignored the demand.

Critics of the war appeared long before the attack began on March 19. Some said the proof of Saddam possessing WMDs was too weak. Others worried that America would be forced to remain in Iraq for years to keep the peace. By staying in Iraq, the Americans would risk making more enemies in the region. That was the concern of the secretary of state. In fact, Colin Powell later said, "I tried to avoid this war. . . . I took [Bush] through the consequences of going into an Arab country and becoming the occupiers." No country wants to be controlled by a foreign army, and it was not hard to predict that Muslims would be particularly upset about being ruled by non-Muslims. Bush and some of his aides dismissed these worries. They wanted a change of regime in Iraq—an end to Saddam Hussein and his tyrannical ways. They also still claimed the Iraqi leader could one day arm terrorists with WMDs.

An Easy Victory?

The Iraq War began with missile and bombing strikes on military targets. Within hours, British and U.S. troops entered Iraq on their way to Baghdad. In less than three weeks the coalition forces reached the capital, but by that time Saddam and his top aides were hiding. The first troops did not find any WMDs, but

Baghdad burns from missile and bombing strikes from the first wave of attacks in March 2003.

the search for them went on for years. Indeed the United States never found any of the weapons Bush and his aides had claimed Saddam possessed. Some Americans believed Bush had lied to lead the country into another war when the focus should have remained on Afghanistan. Bush and his aides said they acted on what they believed to be true.

The Bush administration made bad decisions in the first few months of its occupation. One of these was disbanding the Iraqi army and banning Saddam's political supporters from positions in the new government. Many of the soldiers became **insurgents** who fought U.S. troops and the new Iraqi government the Americans helped create. And Saddam's political supporters had key skills that did not exist among those Iraqis who for years had been excluded from administrative positions.

But the depth of the problem to come was not clear on May 1, 2003. That's when President Bush greeted U.S. sailors on the aircraft carrier *Abraham Lincoln*. He told them and the world, "Major combat operations in Iraq have ended. In the battle of Iraq, the United States and our allies have prevailed [won]." The coalition would now begin to rebuild Iraq and help the country become a democracy.

But by August, Bush aides could see that that insurgency was building. Iraqis who disliked the U.S. presence were carrying out attacks against coalition forces. After one deadly attack, Bush said, "Terrorists want us to retreat and we cannot. We need to redouble our efforts against terror." The insurgents would soon include foreigners with ties to Al Qaeda. Iraq had not supported bin Laden, but now the country was the main battleground in the war on terror. In the months ahead, Bush admitted that the U.S. faced problems in Iraq. But he still believed that the invasion had been the right thing to do and that the activities of the coalition forces would help bring peace to the country.

OTHER CONCERNS

While the fighting in Iraq dominated the news, Bush tried to address other issues both at home and overseas. One involved Medicare, the government health plan for the elderly. At the end of 2003, Bush signed a law designed to pay for many medicines used by people on the plan. Some Democrats, however, feared that the new law would not reduce the overall cost of the drugs, which was a concern for many Americans. Bush also promoted "faith-based" social-service programs, as he had in Texas, so that religious groups could use federal money to help the needy.

"Mission Accomplished"

President Bush had helped fly the military plane that brought him aboard the USS *Abraham Lincoln*. Upon landing on the deck, he jumped out of the aircraft wearing the suit a military pilot would wear. Bush looked like one of the troops he praised so often. When the president spoke that day, he stood in front of a banner that read "Mission Accomplished." The sailors on the *Lincoln* had asked to put it up, to show that their part of the Iraqi War was over. But Bush chose to stand in front of it, suggesting to many Americans that he also thought the broader mission—fighting in Iraq—had been accomplished. The image would become famous as the war went on and thousands of American troops were killed in Iraq. To opponents of the war, it suggested that Bush and his aides had not prepared for what would happen after the invasion.

Soon after the war in Iraq started, Bush approved a second tax cut. At almost the same time, he requested billions of dollars to fight that war and for antiterrorism operations in Pakistan. His presidency would see a previous budget surplus disappear. Instead, the government would spend more money than it took in, with fewer taxes collected and more money spent overseas. That imbalance created what is called a **deficit**. The overall debt also began to grow, and the country would have to pay interest on the money it borrowed. Bush's policies angered some conservatives, who opposed the growing debt and overall government spending. At the end of 2003, Bush said he would drastically cut the deficit in coming years. Economic experts doubted his plan, and Democratic senator Kent Conrad of North Dakota said that when it came to the economy, the administration was "all spin, all the time." This was an indirect way of saying that the government tried to draw favorable conclusions from facts that didn't justify a rosy outlook.

Some of the federal money went into new programs to help Africa. Bush's policy there won wide support. Many nations of that continent faced poverty and a growing problem with AIDS. Bush called for billions of dollars to fight the viral disease.

As 2004 began, Bush told Americans that the hundreds of thousands of U.S. troops in Iraq and Afghanistan were "bringing hope" and "making America more secure." The recession had ended and the economy was growing stronger. The Department of Homeland Security was watching for new terrorists threats. And the country had survived difficult times and was moving forward. Bush said, "The cause we serve is right, because it is the cause of all mankind."

But Bush would face another tough year during 2004, as the war in Iraq worsened and he sought a second term as president.

Four More Years

As George W. Bush knew from his experience and that of his father, U.S. presidential campaigns are long. Bush began preparing to run again in the middle of 2003, yet he told reporters he was still focused on the country's major issues: the economy and the war in Iraq. A number of Democrats hoped to run against him in 2004; Senator John Kerry of Massachusetts finally won his party's nomination. In 2003 Kerry wrote in his book *A Call to Service*, "Those who seek to lead have a duty to . . . make Americans safer . . . [and] more trusted and respected in the world." Kerry had supported the invasion of Iraq, but he thought Bush's policies had weakened trust and respect for the United States.

The War Goes On

President Bush received good news at the end of 2003, when U.S. forces captured Saddam Hussein. He would be put on trial in 2005 and found guilty of "crimes against humanity," including killing his own people. The former Iraqi leader would be executed in 2006. But the arrest of Saddam did not end the insurgency. Instead, it grew, leading to more U.S. casualties during 2004.

The end of 2003 also brought the first reports on how the United States treated its foreign prisoners. Hundreds of people captured in Afghanistan sat in cells at the U.S. Naval base at Guantánamo, Cuba. The Bush administration refused to bring them to trial, and many of the prisoners said they were not part

of Al Qaeda or the Taliban. The United States also had prisoners in Afghanistan in jails run by the CIA. Through 2004 news reports suggested that the prisoners there and elsewhere were being tortured.

In January 2004 the U.S. military began to investigate activities at an Iraqi prison called Abu Ghraib. Pictures of U.S. soldiers abusing prisoners there soon emerged, followed by evidence of abuse and torture at other prisons. Bush later insisted, "We do not torture." But earlier he had approved the use of waterboarding, a technique that makes prisoners feel as if they are drowning. Most legal experts agree that waterboarding is a form of torture.

The details of the treatment of prisoners came out slowly. Voters did not know the full story during the 2004 campaign. But long after Bush had said the main military operations were over, many knew that the Iraq War was not going well. Osama bin Laden was still on the loose. And Bush seemed to ignore Democrats or any criticisms of his policies. Just before the election, voters were split on whether Bush was a uniter, as he had once claimed. According to the results of one poll, 48 percent called him a uniter, but the same number said that he was dividing the country.

ANOTHER VICTORY

Iraq and the war on terrorism were the focus of the 2004 presidential campaign. Bush insisted, "Iraq is a central part of the war on terror." Kerry said the country's focus should be on rebuilding Afghanistan and finding bin Laden. The war in Iraq, the senator said, had actually created more terrorism, as Arabs

THE CYCLING PRESIDENT

Always athletic, George W. Bush often took daily runs as a young man. During his presidency, a knee injury forced him to switch to riding a bike instead. He often went for hour-long rides on a special course owned by the U.S. government. Bush also took time to ride while on foreign trips and at his ranch in Texas. Pedaling at top speed, he would easily race past the Secret Service men who rode nearby to protect him. He also rode once with Lance Armstrong, one of the top cyclists in the world. Friends saw his fast pace as part of his desire to compete—and win. Running and riding helped Bush stay in shape. But these physical activities also helped him deal with the many problems he faced as president. He said in 2002, "You tend to forget everything that's going on in your mind and just concentrate on the time, distance or the sweat."

sought to hurt the United States because they were angry about the country's actions. Many Americans believed this, yet polls showed that they still trusted Bush more when it came to combating terrorism. Bush said, "I've shown the American people I know how to lead."

The final results that November were close. Bush won just over 50 percent of the popular vote. And once again, one state was the key in deciding the winner. This time it was Ohio. Some people in that midwestern state reported problems with the voting process, as in Florida in 2000. But Kerry accepted the results without any legal challenge. Bush claimed he had won political "capital," or the kind of support that would let him forge ahead with his plans. "I earned capital . . . and now I intend to spend it."

PLANS FOR THE SECOND TERM

On January 20, 2005, Bush began his second term. His speech that day discussed freedom, and the role of the United States in helping to spread it. "It is the policy of the United States to seek and support the growth of democratic movements and institutions in every nation and culture, with the ultimate goal of ending tyranny in our world." Some Americans praised the speech, but others thought that Bush ignored several facts. The country had close ties with nations, such as Saudi Arabia, that were not democratic and might never be. And seeking to spread democracy around the world was a large task. America was still struggling to build democracy in Iraq. No one knew whether Bush would succeed there. What would it cost, in money or military might, to take on more nations?

President George W. Bush delivers his inaugural address on January 20, 2005, pledging to spread freedom and to heal divisions, such as those over the war in Iraq.

BATTLES ALL AROUND

Despite frequent questions about the advisability of his actions, Bush was convinced that he was succeeding in Iraq. And he wanted to make big changes at home too. He wanted to spend his political capital on strengthening Social Security, the government-run aid plan that provides money for the elderly and others with little or no income. Social Security was a matter of great concern because without major changes in its operation or funding, the program would run out of money in a few decades. Bush wanted to let those who wished to do so use their own money to invest in retirement plans.

Democrats in Congress told Bush they opposed his plan, but he pushed forward. He toured the country for two months, trying to win support for his private-investment plan. Many elderly people did not want any changes. They feared they could actually lose money under Bush's plan. Some Democrats just refused to help Bush on this important issue, as they had with tax cuts, the war, and No Child Left Behind. They were tired of how he ignored their views. They helped organize groups to oppose the plan. When the president finished his tour, Americans liked his Social Security plan less than when he started. Bush saw he would not get the votes he needed for his plan. He had won the election but lost his first political battle. The second term would continue to present Bush with many challenges.

Iraq was still the largest of the challenges, and in June 2005 the president again talked about the war. The government had officially declared that Saddam had not had weapons of mass destruction. Bush, however, said that the war was still important for bringing democracy to Iraq and perhaps other parts of the Middle East. But critics said, as John Kerry had noted during the campaign of 2004, that the U.S. invasion of Iraq had brought the terrorists there. And some of the people fighting U.S. and Iraqi troops were not terrorists, but Iraqi citizens who hated the ongoing occupation.

In June Bush said he would not send more troops to Iraq. About 150,000 men and women were already there. The number of troops in Iraq had been an issue since before the start of the war. One U.S. general had requested more troops than Bush wanted to send. The military went with the lower number, and critics said it was not enough to fight the insurgency that had developed in the summer of 2003. In any event, American support for the war had continued to fall since the early success at the time of the initial invasion.

A Deadly Storm

In August 2005 Bush went to his ranch in Crawford, Texas, as he often did during the summer. At the end of the month, a powerful hurricane named Katrina roared across the Gulf of Mexico and slammed into several states. New Orleans, Louisiana, was particularly hard hit. Special dams called levees broke, allowing 20 feet of water to flood most of the city. Tens of thousands of people, many of them poor African Americans,

The aftermath of Hurricane Katrina in 2005 was a flooded and devastated New Orleans, Lousiana.

were forced to flee their homes, and more than a thousand died. As the crisis went on, some New Orleans residents and African Americans elsewhere in the country said that the government was too slow to respond. The president was criticized for waiting several days to come to New Orleans, and then simply flying over the city, instead of touching down and offering a personal message to the survivors and first responders. At a time when several thousand displaced people were housed inside a sports arena with little

THE PRESIDENT AND THE COURTS

Under the Constitution, presidents name judges to federal courts, though the Senate must approve the nominees. George W. Bush chose a large number of conservative judges, ones likely to support his views on such issues as helping businesses, reducing access to abortions, and limiting the rights of criminal defendants and convicted criminals. Conservatives say that when thinking about whether a given law is constitutional, they try to follow the "original intent" of the leaders who wrote the Constitution. Some of the greatest impact of the presidency of George W, Bush is associated with the Supreme Court. In September 2005 he nominated John Roberts for the position of chief justice of the United States, or leader of the Court. Several months later he nominated Samuel Alito as an associate justice. Both men hold conservative views; those of Alito were more conservative than the rulings of the justice he replaced. Justices serve for life, so Bush's appointments could shape key legal issues for years to come.

food or water, the president said that the government official in charge of the emergency help was doing a "heck of a job."

The government seemed to have not prepared for the storm, and the response of most federal agencies in the aftermath was slow. African American anger was particularly strong. Barack Obama, then a U.S. senator from Illinois, said the government was "detached from the realities of inner city life in a place like New Orleans." Many poor people did not have cars to get out of the city or money to stay in hotels if they could not stay with friends. As September went on, Bush announced that the government would spend billions of dollars to help the homeless and rebuild the city. But the Katrina disaster weakened Bush's earlier image as a strong, bold leader.

Iraq: The Constant Problem

For decades, presidents have addressed the nation from the Oval Office of the White House. On December 18, 2005, Bush gave his first Oval Office speech since the start of the Iraq War over two years before. More than two thousand Americans had now been killed in Iraq, most of them after Bush had told the nation that major military operations were over. By some counts, 25,000 Iraqi civilians had also been killed. Bush stressed that good things were happening in Iraq, as another election had just taken place there. But he also said, "The work in Iraq has been especially difficult—more difficult than we expected." And he admitted that "much of the intelligence turned out to be wrong"— referring to the intelligence he had once said made the war necessary. Still, invading Iraq had been the right thing to do to remove Saddam. And continuing the war was important to make sure that terrorists did not use Iraq as a base.

Protesters walk to an antiwar demonstration in front of the White House in September 2005.

By this time, more Americans were opposing the war. In September at least` 100,000 protesters came to Washington, D.C., demanding the war's end. This protest and others like it were the largest in the United States since those against the Vietnam War. Yet many Americans still supported Bush and war, though not as many as two years before. One Bush supporter said, "If troops come home now, then all of the sons that are dead are dead for nothing and nothing is going to be finished."

As Americans debated the war, some also questioned whether Bush had acted illegally in the fight against terrorism. In December, the media reported on a secret program to listen in on certain phone calls without legal permission. The U.S. agency involved also read some people's e-mail messages. Bush had secretly signed an executive order to create this program in 2002. Bush said he had powers under the Constitution as commander in chief to order this domestic spying.

Bush said the program dealt only with "the interception of international communications of people with known links to Al Qaeda and related terrorist organizations." A day earlier, he had called the program "a vital tool in our war against the terrorists. It is critical to saving American lives."

But some legal experts said that Bush had been wrong to claim that his powers as commander in chief allowed him to set up the program. The domestic spying, critics said, was illegal. And later reports showed that the government had worked with

U.S. phone companies to collect the domestic telephone records of millions of Americans. The government was not just focusing on international communication or suspected terrorists, as Bush had claimed. The issue highlighted the difficulty the country faced as it battled terrorism. The government needs information on terrorists, but Americans also want to know that their leaders obey the laws and that their privacy is secure.

DIFFICULT TIMES

For the first time, Bush began to admit to Americans that he and his administration had made some mistakes. But his critics were still unhappy. By now, even some Republicans were questioning the president's policies. In a meeting with some conservatives, party leaders told Bush and his aides that it was wrong to say that things were going well in Iraq. One conservative critic was unhappy with the growing debt, as the cost of the two wars continued to rise. But Bush still believed he was doing the right thing for the nation.

Few people saw the more emotional side of President Bush. Everyone knew about his jokes and the nicknames he gave to everyone he met. They saw his confidence—or arrogance—as he laid out his plans. But in private, Bush could easily cry when he learned of people who had made sacrifices or taken heroic action. He often met soldiers wounded in Iraq and fought back tears as they talked. Bush knew he was asking the soldiers to do a difficult job—and one that more Americans now believed was not worth the cost. Bush saw that firsthand, too. On one hospital visit, a wounded soldier's parent blamed the president for her son's serious injuries. Bush felt the woman's anger and later said, "I don't blame her." But the war would go on, because Bush believed it was the only way to keep America safe.

A DIFFICULT END *Seven*

$\mathcal{G}$oing into 2006 George W. Bush heard the growing complaints about his presidency. Some Democrats thought he should fire his secretary of defense, Donald Rumsfeld. But just as Bush expected loyalty from others, he defended the people who worked for him. In April he said Rumsfeld was doing a fine job and rejected calls to fire him. Bush said, "I'm the decider, and I decide what is best." To Bush and his supporters, being "the decider" was part of a president's duties, and Bush believed in his ability to make good decisions. But his opponents had another view: Bush too often ignored facts or well-supported opinions when he made his decisions. He appeared stubborn, and too often, his decisions were not good ones.

Throughout most of his presidency, Bush counted on strong support from Republicans in Congress. But by 2006 some of that support was weakening. Immigration was one issue that divided the Republican Party. As governor of Texas, Bush had seen how important Hispanic workers were to the economy, even though many had entered the country illegally. As president, Bush knew that some illegal immigrants committed crimes or needed government services. But most, he said, "are decent people who work hard, support their families, practice their faith, and lead responsible lives." Bush supported a plan to help many illegal immigrants become citizens. At the same time, he planned to add six thousand new Border Patrol agents to prevent people without the necessary documents from entering the country illegally. Some Republicans believed that the immigrants took away jobs from

Americans or used services to which they weren't entitled. These Republicans opposed the effort to give citizenship to illegal immigrants already in the country.

Still Struggling in Iraq

For most of his presidency, Bush relied on Republican control of Congress to ensure the passage of laws he favored. The election of 2006 saw the Democrats take control of both houses of Congress. The election seemed to reflect many Americans' growing dislike of the president and his policies, especially in Iraq. His popularity in polls had fallen to less than 40 percent, the worst of his presidency.

Before the election, comments from the military and intelligence agencies showed how badly the war in Iraq was going, despite the president's public statements in support of his policies. In August General John Abizaid told Congress that the violence in Iraq at the time was about as bad as he had seen. Now Iraqis were not just battling the Americans and the government they helped create. Iraqis were fighting among themselves on the basis of the form of Islam they followed. Although the majority of the world's Muslims are Sunni, this is not true in Iraq, where followers of Shia Islam are the most numerous. Armed members of the two groups fought each other, and Muslims from other countries poured into Iraq to stir the violence. Abizaid said if the killing was not stopped, "it is possible that Iraq could move toward civil war."

The next month, an intelligence report denied a claim Bush had repeatedly asserted: that the war in Iraq was making the United States safer from terrorism. The new report said more

A Powerful Vice President

George W. Bush's loss of support was matched by his vice president's. Many people argued that Dick Cheney was the most powerful vice president ever. Some experts even called him a "co-president" with Bush, though Bush always denied the charge. Cheney and his staff played a large role in shaping the U.S. response to terrorism and in the decision to go to war 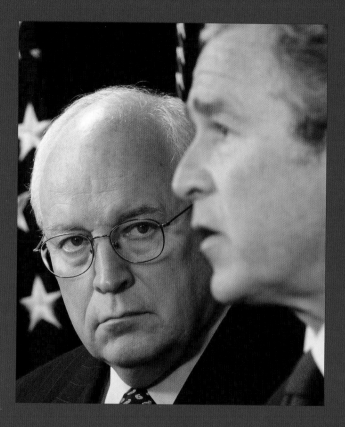 with Iraq. The vice president often made the strongest statements about the threat Saddam Hussein posed, even after facts had proved Cheney's claims wrong. During his time as vice president, Cheney also pushed for policies that helped businesses, especially oil companies. And he tried to expand the president's powers as much as possible, while taking away some power from Congress.

Muslims were eager to fight a jihad, or "holy war" against Americans. "If this trend continues, threats to U.S. interests at home and abroad will become more diverse, leading to increasing attacks worldwide."

As 2007 began, Bush announced that he was sending more than 20,000 additional troops to Iraq. Their mission was to help end the violence in Baghdad and other areas. Meanwhile, the Americans would continue to train Iraqi police and soldiers so the Americans could later come home for good. The extra troops and their supporting weapons were said to provide a surge in an effort to tame the violence. In the months that followed, American deaths rose, but then began to fall. The additional troops did help end some of the violence against civilians. So did several other factors. The Americans began to receive help from Sunni groups in Iraq who opposed the foreign terrorists. And a powerful Shia leader told his armed forces to stop their violent activities. But in politics, the different Iraqi groups still found it hard to work together.

A Weakened Economy

Back in the United States, the president faced new concerns about the economy. Conditions had improved after the recession, but now the economy was beginning to slow again. The major concern was the health of large financial companies. By the end of 2007, some firms were losing large amounts of money because of bad mortgage loans. Bush, like Bill Clinton before him, had welcomed a rise in home ownership. But many of the loans had gone to people who could not afford to make the necessary payments regularly. For years, the value of homes had risen sharply. Now they began to fall. At the same time, many

In early 2008 the housing crisis continued to grow as homeowners defaulted on their loans, leading to bank foreclosures.

families could no longer repay their loans. Banks and other financial companies lost money and became less able to make new loans. Bush said, "The government's got a role to play, but it is limited," as he argued that the overall economy was still strong. He did say that a government housing agency would try to help some families change their mortgages so they wouldn't lose their homes.

Going into 2008, however, the housing crisis continued to grow. The value of homes kept falling, particularly in states where selling prices had risen quickly in previous years. Yet people looking to buy their first homes found it harder to get a loan. Home building slowed, so construction workers lost jobs. People bought fewer appliances and other items needed in new homes, so stores saw their sales fall.

Bush took action in January 2008, as the government approved a plan to send checks to taxpayers. The hope was that people would spend the money and help improve the economy. The next month Bush said the country was not facing a recession. But the economic crisis continued to spread as several large banks failed.

By the fall the economy was reaching a crisis. Bush now wanted to use government money to help large financial companies survive. He said in September 2008, "Without immediate action by Congress, America could slip into a financial panic . . . our entire economy is in danger." Some Americans from both parties, however, thought the government should not help large financial companies, which had caused many of their own economic problems as they pursued higher profits. Still, in October, Congress approved a bill that set aside $700 billion to help struggling financial companies. Later some money also went to General Motors and Chrysler, two of the country's three major carmakers.

Wall Street vs. Main Street

When discussing the U.S. economy, political experts sometimes focus on two major groups. "Wall Street" refers to the large banks and investment companies centered near New York City's financial area, often designated by the name of one of its principal streets. "Main Street" refers to smaller businesses and average workers around the country. As the economy worsened in 2008, many Americans became angry, thinking the government was doing too much to help Wall Street and not enough to help Main Street. Part of the anger was due to the huge bonuses financial companies gave some of their highest-paid officers, who might receive millions of dollars each year, even if the companies did not do well. In some cases, companies that received part of the $700 billion from the government still paid the bonuses. The companies said they had to honor contracts they had signed with their top employees. But on Main Street, average Americans could not understand rewarding executives who had almost caused their companies' failure. Even worse, the bonuses came when millions of Americans were losing their jobs or their homes.

Another Growing Problem

Going into 2008, the surge in Iraq seemed to be reducing the violence there. The year before had seen the most U.S. deaths since the start of the war, and in March the total reached four thousand. But the number of monthly insurgent attacks had begun to fall. Now President Bush had to focus on major troubles in

Afghanistan. Although the Taliban had been forced from power, many active members were still in the region. So was Al Qaeda, which built new camps in the mountains of Pakistan. Fighters based in these camps were able to carry out attacks on U.S. and international forces in Afghanistan.

Bombing attacks against U.S. and international forces had begun to increase in 2006 and continued to grow. As in Iraq, some attacks killed civilians as well. The Taliban used money from the sale of opium to finance their war. The drug comes from the poppy flower and is then turned into heroin, a strong illegal drug. Going into 2007 the Taliban increased its influence in parts of Afghanistan. U.S. forces and their allies killed more insurgents, but more Americans died in the fighting as well. At times, the United States bombed villages where the Taliban were thought to live and accidentally killed civilians. This increased Afghan anger against the Americans. The United States had better success using remote-controlled planes to hunt down and kill Al Qaeda leaders in Pakistan.

In March 2008 Bush told soldiers in Afghanistan that they were "on the front lines of helping this young democracy succeed." But many experts wondered whether the government there could ever function well. President Hamid Karzai did not have broad support, and in April insurgents attempted to kill him. Some Pakistanis were known to be in Afghanistan, helping the Taliban and Al Qaeda. And few U.S. allies in Afghanistan were actively fighting the insurgents. In the United States, Bush's critics said he had made a major error by focusing so much on Iraq. Afghanistan was the true center of the war on terror, and the administration had not paid enough attention to events there after 2002.

A Regional Power

As the United States fought wars in Iraq and Afghanistan, President Bush had to pay increasing attention to the nation that sits between them—Iran. Since 1979, Iran had been ruled by a conservative Shia Muslim government that opposed the United States and its policies in the Middle East. Bush knew that Iran offered support to Shia Iraqis battling the coalition. In 2007 Bush learned that Iran had a secret program to build nuclear weapons. The Iranians hoped to make one to fit on missiles that could deliver it to targets across the Middle East. These included sites in Israel, a strong U.S. ally in the region. Iran's leaders had said Israel controlled land that belonged to the Palestinians and the country had no right to exist. Iran had stopped its nuclear weapons program, the CIA believed, but it could quickly start again. Bush did not want a hostile nation such as Iran armed with such deadly weapons. But the president did not want to start another war. He called for international pressure on Iran, such as limits on trade, to force it to end the weapons program. The Iranians, however, refused to stop making the material needed to construct nuclear weapons.

Coming to the End

Under the Constitution, a U.S. president can serve only two terms. As 2008 went on, George W. Bush knew that a new president would have to tackle the many problems the country faced. As Republicans prepared for the election, many of them did not want Bush to help them raise campaign funds.

The candidates did not want to be associated with Bush's policies, which were now unpopular across much of the country. Republican voters still largely supported Bush, but most Democrats and independents did not.

In November, Democratic senator Barack Obama defeated Republican senator John McCain for the presidency. Obama talked often about the need for change after eight difficult years under George W. Bush. In the two months before Obama was inaugurated, the economy continued to worsen. In Iraq, the government there called for all U.S. troops to leave the country by the end of 2011. Bush had said U.S. troops would leave as Iraq's military and police could better protect the country.

The media covered the presidential victory of Barack Obama in November 2008.

He had pulled out some troops before the election. In Afghanistan, the Taliban was still strong, though some experts thought more U.S. troops—another surge—could end some of the violence. By this point, more than 30,000 U.S. troops were already there, with more planned to arrive. No one knew, however, when U.S. troops would leave. One expert feared Afghanistan's central government would never be strong enough to completely wipe out the Taliban or other rebels.

When Bush's term ended in January 2009, he and Laura moved to Dallas, Texas. According to one poll, his approval rating among voters was just 22 percent—the lowest ever recorded for a president leaving office. Americans thought Bush had done well in fighting terrorism. But they did not approve of his policies

Former president George W. Bush salutes as he and First Lady Laura Bush head to a marine helicopter in January 2009.

in Iraq, and they were dissatisfied with his measures aimed at strengthening the economy. Tax cuts and huge expenses for the war had greatly added to the country's debt, and it was still in the middle of what was now called the Great Recession.

JUDGING A DIFFICULT PRESIDENCY

Both George W. Bush and historians had already talked about how future Americans would see him and his presidency. In 2007 he told a reporter, "I made the decision to lead . . . the fundamental question is, Is the world better off as a result of your leadership?" Bush believed his actions helped the United States and the world—especially his forcing Saddam Hussein from power. But the world might not know for years whether invading Iraq had been good for that country and the region. The war in Afghanistan could also drag on.

Many reporters covered Bush during his years as governor of Texas and as president. They saw that he was friendly, intelligent, and quick to make decisions. But many also thought he refused to admit mistakes or listen to people with ideas that didn't match his. Even some former members of his administration believed that Bush and his staff at the White House did not look for facts before making decisions. Bush himself said he was "a gut player." He trusted what he felt or believed rather than waiting for solid information. That trait weakened his presidency, though in his last two years, he did seem willing to listen to and work with others. By then, though, he was deeply unpopular and no longer had the power to get what he wanted, as he had right after September 11.

To some experts, the treatment of suspected terrorists during the Bush administration was one of the president's biggest failures. In addition, the administration's denial of the legal rights of some detainees was overturned more than once by the U.S. Supreme Court. Bush ignored international law and advice from military lawyers when he approved torture. His defenders said Bush did what he felt was necessary to protect the country. In the end, though, even the president of the United States is expected to obey the law. Justice Sandra Day O'Connor, of the Supreme Court, said that even during wartime, presidents cannot do whatever they want "when it comes to the rights of the Nation's citizens."

Bush's many problems during his presidency sometimes hid things most people agree he did well. He tried to tackle the difficult issue of illegal immigration in a fair way. He called for billions of dollars to fight AIDS in Africa. He helped unite and calm Americans after the horrible terrorist attacks of September 11. Despite some problems with No Child Left Behind, the program has helped raise some test scores.

As Bush left office, historians agreed that they would need decades to truly judge his presidency. Former administration members would reveal what they knew, and government records would be released. But this is certain: Bush faced several major crises. He followed his conservative ideas of how to best run the country. He angered many Americans along the way, especially by acting secretly and seemingly lying to the nation. But he remained convinced that he had done the best he could to improve the United States and the world.

The presidency of George W. Bush consisted of problems and failures, but also issues he handled well. Many historians agree that it will take many years before a true judgment of his presidency can take place.

1946
George W. Bush is born on July 6 in New Haven, Connecticut

1964
Graduates from Phillips Academy in Andover, Massachusetts

1968
Graduates from Yale University

1975
Receives master's degree from Harvard University

1977
Marries Laura Welch

1989
With other business partners, buys the Texas Rangers baseball team

1940

1994
Becomes the governor of
Texas

1998
Wins reelection as governor
of Texas

2000
Is elected forty-third president
of the United States

2004
Is elected to second
presidential term

2009
Ends second term as
president and leaves office

2010

NOTES

CHAPTER ONE

p. 7, "You just don't hit a building like that." George W. Bush, quoted in Robert Draper, *Dead Certain: The Presidency of George W. Bush.* New York: Free Press, 2007, p. 135.

p. 7, "A second plane. . . . America is under attack." Andrew Card, quoted in Bob Woodward, *Bush at War.* New York: Simon & Schuster, 2002, p. 15.

p. 8, "Freedom itself. . . . will be defended." George W. Bush, "Bush: U.S. Military on 'High Alert,'" CNN, 12 September, 2001. Available online at http://archives.cnn.com/2001/US/09/11/bush.second.statement. (Accessed 12 October 2009.)

p. 8, "War president." George W. Bush, "Transcript for February 8," *Meet the Press*, 13 February 2004. Available online at www.msnbc.msn.com/id/4179618/. (Accessed 13 October 2009.)

p. 12, "A natural leader and a good guy to be with." David Alan Richards, quoted in Nicholas D. Kristoff, "Ally of an Older Generation Amid the Tumult of the '60s," *New York Times*, 19 June 2000. Available online at www.nytimes.com/library/politics/camp/061900wh-bush.html. (Accessed 13 October 2009.)

p. 13, "I just don't remember. . . . I wasn't much of a protester." George W. Bush, quoted in "In His Own Words: 'Leadership Comes in All Forms,'" *Washington Post*, 27 July 1999. Available online at www.washingtonpost.com/wp-srv/politics/campaigns/wh2000/stories/bushtext072799.htm. (Accessed 14 October 2009.)

p. 14, "I was prepared to go." George W. Bush, quoted in George Lardner Jr. and Lois Romano, "At Height of Vietnam, Bush Picks Guard," *Washington Post*, 28 July 1999. Available online at www.washingtonpost.com/wp-srv/politics/campaigns/wh2000/stories/bush072899.htm. (Accessed 14 October 2009.)

p. 15, "There are some people. . . . the way it was." George W. Bush, quoted in Jo Thomas, "After Yale, Bush Ambled Amiably Into His Future," *The New York Times*, 22 July 2000. Available online at www.nytimes.com/library/politics/camp/072200wh-bush.html. (Accessed 14 October 2009.)

p. 15, "He was very good . . . getting things done." Michael E. Porter, quoted in John Solomon, "Bush, Harvard Business School and the Makings of a President," *The New York Times*, 18 June 2000. Available online at www.nytimes.com/2000/06/18/business/bush-harvard-business-school-and-the-makings-of-a-president.html?pagewanted=2. (Accessed 15 October 2009.)

CHAPTER TWO

p. 16, "Federal government . . . our lives." George W. Bush, quoted in Lardner and Romano, "Young Bush, a Political Natural, Revs Up." (Accessed 16 October 2009.)

p. 17, "In a lot of ways . . . known him that well." Laura Bush, quoted in George Lardner Jr. and Lois Romano, "Young Bush, a Political Natural, Revs Up," *Washington Post*, 29 July 1999. Available online at www.washingtonpost.com/wp-srv/politics/campaigns/wh2000/stories/bush072999.htm. (Accessed 16 October 2009.)

p. 18, "Free enterprise, the philosophy of growth." George W. Bush, quoted in Lardner and Romano, "Young Bush, a Political Natural, Revs Up." (Accessed 16 October 2009.)

p. 18, "Today is . . . a real farm." George W. Bush, quoted in Nicholas D. Kristoff, "Learning How to Run: A West Texas Stumble," *The New York Times*, 27 July 2000. Available online at www.nytimes.com/library/politics/camp/072700wh-bush-lubbock.html. (Accessed 16 October 2009.)

p. 20, "I'm not going to pretend. . . . a fair shake." George W. Bush, quoted in George Lardner Jr. and Lois Romano, "Bush Name Helps Fuel Oil Dealings," *Washington Post*, 30 July 1999. Available online at www.washingtonpost.com/wp-srv/politics/campaigns/wh2000/stories/bush073099.htm. (Accessed 16 October 2009.)

p. 20, "Recommit my heart to Jesus Christ." George W. Bush, *A Charge to Keep*. New York: Morrow, 1999, p. 136.

p. 21, "Eyes and ears . . . what was going on." James A. Baker, quoted in Nicholas D. Kristoff, "For Bush, Thrill Was in Father's Chase," *The New York Times*, 29 August 2000. Available online at www.nytimes.com/library/politics/camp/082900wh-bush.html. (Accessed 19 October 2009.)

p. 22, "You need to do . . . your own reputation." Roland Betts, quoted in George Lardner Jr. and Lois Romano, "Bush Moves Up to the Majors," *Washington Post*, 31 July 1999. Available online at www.washingtonpost.com/wp-srv/politics/campaigns/wh2000/stories/bush073199.htm. (Accessed 19 October 2009.)

p. 23, "Hey . . . some bubble gum?" George W. Bush, quoted in Draper, *Dead Certain*, p. 41.

p. 25, "Strong emotions . . . get whipped." George W. Bush, quoted in Frank Bruni, *Ambling into History*. New York: HarperCollins, 2002, p. 140.

CHAPTER THREE

p. 26, "She wanted to make sure . . . really wanted to do." George W. Bush, quoted in Lardner and Romano, "Bush Moves Up to the Majors."

p. 27, "Dependency on government . . . our very future." Bush, *A Charge to Keep*, p. 25.

p. 27, "Had that engine failed, I could have been killed." George W. Bush, quoted in Sam Howe Verhovek, "Governor and Her Rival Meet in Debate," *The New York Times*, 22 October 1994. Available online at www.nytimes.com/1994/10/22/us/the-1994-campaign-texas-governor-and-her-rival-meet-in-debate.html. (Accessed 20 October 2009.)

p. 28, "Only for a weak person." George W. Bush, quoted in Draper, *Dead Certain*, p. 50.

p. 29, "First and foremost . . . the state of Texas." George W. Bush, quoted in "Bush's Environmental Record," Online NewsHour, 22 August, 2000. Available online at www.pbs.org/newshour/bb/election/july-dec00/bush_environment_8-22.html. (Accessed 20 October 2009.)

p. 30, "What government cannot do. . . . a higher authority." George W. Bush, quoted in Grant Williams, "The Bush Brand of Charity," *The Chronicle of Philanthropy*, 6 April 2000. Available online at http://philanthropy.com/free/articles/v12/i12/12000101.htm. (Accessed 21 October 2009.)

p. 31, "If administered . . . will save other innocent lives." Bush, *A Charge to Keep*, p. 147.

p. 31, "I had done . . . the laws of Texas." Bush, *A Charge to Keep*, p. 155.

p. 31, "There is no chance. . . . a very bad man." Bush, *A Charge to Keep*, p. 164.

p. 33, "From accepting responsibility. . . . less and less." Bush, *A Charge to Keep*, p. 229.

p. 33, "That does not mean. . . . effective means of help." Bush, *A Charge to Keep*, p. 230.

p. 34, "Put food on your family . . . admissions." George W. Bush, quoted in Bruni, *Ambling into History*, p. 39.

CHAPTER FOUR

p. 37, "I'm going to need . . . make good decisions." George W. Bush, quoted in Draper, *Dead Certain*, p. 89.

p. 38, "So much promise. . . . It is a time for new beginnings." George W. Bush, quoted in "Gov. George W. Bush," Online NewsHour, 3 August 2000. Available online at www.pbs.org/newshour/election2000/gopconvention/george_w_bush.html. (Accessed 22 October 2009.)

p. 38, "They're for the powerful, and we're for the people. Al Gore, quoted in "Al Gore, Part III," Online NewsHour, 17 August 2000. Available online at www.pbs.org/newshour/election2000/demconvention/gore3.html. (Accessed on 22 October 2009.)

p. 38, "It will require. . . . to earn your vote." George W. Bush, transcript of the Bush-Gore debate, Commission on Presidential Debates, 3 October 2000. Available online at www.debates.org/index.php?page=october-3-2000-transcript. (Accessed 22 October 2009.)

p. 43, "More than anything. . . . doesn't like a mess." Unidentified friend, quoted in Bruni, *Ambling into History*, p. 208.

p. 43, "Together . . . inspire the American citizens." George W. Bush, quoted in "Bush: 'I Will Give It My All,'" *The Guardian*, 14 December 2000. Available online at www.guardian.co.uk/world/2000/dec/14/uselections2000.usa13. (Accessed 22 October 2009.)

p. 43, "Uniter, not a divider." George W. Bush, quoted in David Horowitz, "'I'm a Uniter, Not a Divider.'" *Salon*, 6 May 1999. Available online at www.salon.com/news/feature/1999/05/06/bush/. (Accessed on 22 October 2009.)

p. 43, "This is my solemn pledge . . . justice and opportunity." George W. Bush, Inaugural address, 20 January 2001. Available online at //www.cnn.com/ALLPOLITICS/inauguration/2001/transcripts/template.html. (Accessed 23 October 2009.)

p. 45, "It was by far . . . in 40 years." Hendrik Hertzberg, quoted in Lou Cannon and Carl M. Cannon, *Reagan's Disciple: George W. Bush's Troubled Quest for a Presidential Legacy*. New York: PublicAffairs Books, 2008, p. 61.

p. 45, "Is needed. . . . our country can afford it." George W. Bush news conference, 22 February 2001. Available online at www.presidency.ucsb.edu/ws/index.php?pid=45948. (Accessed 23 October 2009.)

p. 46, "Crimes against nature." "The Bush Record," *Sierra*, September/October 2004. Available online at www.sierraclub.org/sierra/200409/bush_record_print.asp. (Accessed 23 October 2009.)

p. 49, "Something very, very big. . . . blinking red." George Tenet, quoted in *The 9/11 Commission Report*, National Commission on Terrorist Attacks upon the United States. Available online at http://govinfo.library.unt.edu/911/report/911Report_Exec. htm. (Accessed 23 October 2009.)

CHAPTER FIVE

p. 51, "This enemy hides. . . . won't be able to hide forever." George W. Bush, Remarks of 12 September 2001. Available online at http://avalon.law.yale.edu/sept11/president_054.asp. (Accessed 26 October 2009.)

p. 51, "Either with us . . . with the terrorists." George W. Bush, quoted in *The 9/11 Commission Report*. Available online at http://govinfo.library.unt.edu/911/report/911Report_Ch10.htm. (Accessed 26 October 2009.)

p. 53, "Why. . . . supporting your president!" George W. Bush, quoted in Draper, *Dead Certain*, p. 169.

p. 55, "Axis of evil, aiming to threaten the peace of the world." George W. Bush, State of the Union address, 29 January 2002. Available online at http://usiraq.procon.org/sourcefiles/state.union.2002.pdf. (Accessed 26 October 2009.)

p. 55, "Simply stated. . . . against our allies and against us." Dick Cheney, quoted in "Study: Bush, Aides Made 935 False Statements in Run-up to War." CNN, 24 January 2008. Available online at www.cnn.com/2008/POLITICS/01/23/bush.iraq. (Accessed 26 October 2009.)

p. 56, "Even if . . . time and place of the attack." George W. Bush, quoted in James B. Steinberg, Michael E. O'Hanlon, and Susan E. Rice, *The New National Security Strategy and Preemption*. Brookings Institute Policy Brief Series #113, December 2002. Available online at www.brookings.edu/papers/2002/12terrorism_ohanlon. aspx. (Accessed 26 October 2009.)

p. 56, "(1) defend the national security . . . regarding Iraq." Public Law 107–243, 107th Congress, "Authorization for Use of Military Force Against Iraq Resolution of 2002," 16 October 2002. Available online at www.c-span.org/Content/PDF/hjres114.pdf. (Accessed 27 October 2009.)

p. 57, "I tried to avoid. . . . becoming the occupiers." Colin Powell, quoted in Cannon and Cannon, *Reagan's Disciple*, p. 196.

p. 60, "Major combat operations. . . . and our allies have prevailed" George W. Bush, Remarks of 1 May 2003. Available online at http://usiraq.procon.org/sourcefiles/bush.address.5-1-03.pdf. (Accessed 28 October 2009.)

p. 60, "Terrorists want us. . . . our efforts against terror." George W. Bush, quoted in Bob Woodward, *State of Denial*. New York: Simon & Schuster, 2006, p. 246.

p. 61, "All spin, all the time." Kent Conrad, quoted in Jaime Holguin, "Bush Deficit Plan Draws Derision," CBS News, 17 December 2003. Available online at www.cbsnews. com/stories/2003/12/17/politics/main589170.shtml. (Accessed 27 October 2009.)

p. 61, "Bringing hope . . . more secure." George W. Bush, State of the Union address, 21 January 2004. Available online at www.cnn.com/2004/ALLPOLITICS/01/20/sotu. transcript.1/index.html. (Accessed 27 October 2009.)

p. 61, "The cause we serve . . . the cause of all mankind." George W. Bush, State of the Union address, 21 January 2004. Available online at www.cnn.com/2004/ALL POLITICS/01/20/sotu.transcript.8/index.html. (Accessed 27 October 2009.)

CHAPTER SIX

p. 62, "Those who seek . . . respected in the world." John Kerry, *A Call to Service*. New York: Viking Press, 2003, p. 37.

p. 64, "We do not torture." George W. Bush, quoted in Michael A. Fletcher, "Bush Defends CIA's Clandestine Prisons," *Washington Post*, 8 November 2005. Available online at www.washingtonpost.com/wp-dyn/content/article/2005/11/07/ AR2005110700637.html. (Accessed 9 November 2009.)

p. 64, "Iraq is a central part of the war on terror." George W. Bush, transcript of the Bush-Kerry debate, 30 September 2004. Available online at www.washingtonpost. com/wp-srv/politics/debatereferee/debate_0930.html. (Accessed 9 November 2009.)

p. 65, "You tend to forget . . . the sweat." George W. Bush, quoted in Dana Milbank, "On a Bicycle in Beltsville, Blissfully Unaware," *Washington Post*, 12 May 2005. Available online at www.washingtonpost.com/wp-dyn/content/article/2005/05/11/ AR2005051102170.html. (Accessed 9 November 2009.)

p. 66, "I've shown the American people I know how to lead." George W. Bush, transcript of the Bush-Kerry debate, 30 September 2004. Available online at www. washingtonpost.com/wp-srv/politics/debatereferee/debate_0930.html. (Accessed 9 November 2009.)

p. 66, "I earned capital . . . intend to spend it." George W. Bush, quoted in Chris Suellentrop, "America's New Political Capital," *Slate*, 30 November 2004. Available online at www.slate.com/id/2110256. (Accessed 9 November 2009.)

p. 66, "It is the policy…ending tyranny in our world." George W. Bush, second inaugural address, 20 January 2005. Available online at www.npr.org/templates/story/story. php?storyId=4460172. (Accessed 9 November 2009.)

p. 71, "Heck of a job." George W. Bush, quoted in "'Can I Quit Now?' FEMA Chief Wrote as Katrina Raged," CNN, 3 November 2005. Available online at www.cnn. com/2005/US/11/03/brown.fema.emails/. (Accessed 9 November 2009.)

p. 71, "Detached . . . in a place like New Orleans." Barack Obama, quoted in David Mendell, *Obama: From Promise to Power*. New York: Amistad, 2007, p. 317.

p. 71, "The work in Iraq. . . . turned out to be wrong." George W. Bush, Oval Office address, 18 December 2005. Available online at www.nytimes.com/2005/12/18/ politics/18bush-text.html?pagewanted=3&_r=1. (Accessed 10 November 2009.)

p. 72, "If troops come home now . . . nothing is going to be finished." Unidentified bystander, quoted in "Protesting the War," Online NewsHour, 26 September 2005. Available online at www.pbs.org/newshour/bb/military/july-dec05/protests_9-26. html. (Accessed 10 November 2009.)

p. 72, "The interception . . . related terrorists organizations." George W. Bush, news conference, 19 December 2005. Available online at www.presidency.ucsb.edu/ws/index.php?pid=65077. (Accessed 10 November 2009.)

p. 72, "A vital tool . . . . saving American lives." George W. Bush, radio address, 17 December 2005. Available online at www.presidency.ucsb.edu/ws/index.php?pid=65075. (Accessed 10 November 2009.)

p. 73, "I don't blame her." George W. Bush, quoted in Draper, *Dead Certain*, p. 350.

CHAPTER SEVEN

p. 74, "I'm the decider, and I decide what's best." George W. Bush, quoted in "Bush: 'I'm the Decider' on Rumsfeld," CNN, 18 April 2006. Available online at www.cnn.com/2006/POLITICS/04/18/rumsfeld/. (Accessed 1 December 2009.)

p. 74, "Are decent people . . . and lead responsible lives." George W. Bush, Oval Office address, 15 May 2006. Available online at www.cnn.com/2006/POLITICS/05/15/bush.immigration.text/index.html. (Accessed 1 December 2009.)

p. 75, "It is possible . . . civil war." John Abizaid, quoted in Bob Woodward, *The War Within: A Secret White House History 2006–2008*. New York: Simon & Schuster, 2008, p. 84.

p. 77, "If this trend continues . . . increasing attacks worldwide." National Intelligence Estimate, April 2006, quoted in Gary C. Jacobson, *A Divider, Not a Uniter: George W. Bush and the American People*. New York: Pearson Longman, 2008, p. 287.

p. 79, "The government's got a role to play, but it's limited." George W. Bush, quoted in Mike Allen, "Bush Unveils Mortgage Crisis First Steps," *Politico*, 31 August, 2007. Available online at www.politico.com/news/stories/0807/5581.html. (Accessed 1 December 2009.)

p. 79, Without immediate action . . . is in danger." George W. Bush, quoted in Andrew Rudalevige, "Diminishing Returns: George W. Bush and Congress, 2001–2008," in Robert Maranto, Tom Lansford, and Jeremy Johnson, eds. *Judging Bush*. Stanford, CA: Stanford University Press, 2009, p. 96.

p. 81, "On the front lines…succeed." George W. Bush, quoted in Tabassum Zakaria, "Bush Says If Younger, He Would Work in Afghanistan," Reuters, 13 March 2008. Available online at www.reuters.com/article/idUSN1333111120080313. (Accessed 2 December 2009.)

p. 85, "I made the decision . . . your leadership?" George W. Bush, quoted in Draper, *Dead Certain*, p. 419.

p. 85, "A gut player." George W. Bush, quoted in Woodward, *The War Within*, p. 431.

p. 86, "When it comes to the rights of the nation's citizens." Sandra Day O'Connor, *Hamdi v. Rumsfeld*. Available online at http://caselaw.lp.findlaw.com/scripts/getcase.pl?court=US&vol=000&invol=03-6696#opinion1. (Accessed 2 December 2009.)

GLOSSARY

ballots slips of paper or other items used to record votes in an election

coalition a group of nations united in a common goal, such as fighting an enemy

conservative tending to believe that most old ways are better than new and that the government should play a small role in the economy, grow national social programs more slowly, and build a strong defense

deficit amount of money a government spends that is more than it collects during a given year

delegates people chosen to represent a particular region or group of people at a meeting

fundamentalist person who completely accepts the basic beliefs of a religion

insurgents people fighting to get rid of existing political leaders or a system of government

Islam religion founded by the Prophet Muhammad during the seventh century in what is now Saudi Arabia

liberal tending to believe that the government should play an active role in addressing social and economic problems. Also, a person holding those beliefs.

pardons acts by government officials that release criminals from jail and wipe the crime from their record

United Nations international organization that tries to prevent war and ensure good relations among all countries

Further Information

Books

Crawford, Steve. *War against Terror*. Redding, CT: Brown Bear Books, 2010.

Doak, Robin. *Conflicts in Iraq and Afghanistan*. Milwaukee: World Almanac Library, 2007.

Márquez, Herón. *George W. Bush*. Minneapolis: Twenty-First Century Books, 2007.

Mattern, Joanne. *Laura Bush*. Edina, MN: ABDO Publishing, 2008.

The War in Iraq. New York: Franklin Watts, 2008.

Welch, Catherine A. *George H. W. Bush*. Minneapolis: Lerner Publishing, 2008.

Websites

The American Presidency Project

www.presidency.ucsb.edu/index_docs.php

This site has more than 86,000 documents relating to U.S. presidents, including many for George W. Bush and his father, George H. W. Bush. Statements and documents for the younger Bush include press conferences, radio addresses, inaugural addresses, and executive orders.

The Bush Presidency

www.cbsnews.com/htdocs/politics/bush/framesource.html

At this site, CBS News features keys moments during Bush's second term in office. The site also has links to websites that recap events during his first term and provide information on the Bush family.

Frontline—The Choice 2000

www.pbs.org/wgbh/pages/frontline/shows/choice2000/bush/cron.html

The Public Broadcasting System offers a timeline of events in Bush's life up to the presidential election of 2000, with links to stories providing more information on his background.

United States Election 2000 Web Archive

http://memory.loc.gov/diglib/lcwa/html/elec2000/elec2000-overview. html

The U.S. Library of Congress has collected images from the websites of different news organization that covered the 2000 campaign and the controversial results of the election. Users can choose any of the organizations and a date and see what issues in the campaign were making news that day.

BIBLIOGRAPHY

BOOKS

Bacevich, Andrew J. *The New American Militarism: How Americans Are Seduced by War.* New York: Oxford University Press, 2005.

Barnes, Fred. *Rebel-in-Chief.* New York: Crown Forum, 2006.

Bruni, Frank. *Ambling into History.* New York: HarperCollins, 2002.

Bush, George W. *A Charge to Keep.* New York: Morrow, 1999.

Campbell, Colin, Bert A. Rockman, and Andrew Rudalevige, eds. *The George W. Bush Legacy.* Washington, DC: CQ Press, 2008.

Cannon, Lou, and Carl M. Cannon. *Reagan's Disciple: George W. Bush's Troubled Quest for a Presidential Legacy.* New York: PublicAffairs, 2008.

Draper, Robert. *Dead Certain: The Presidency of George W. Bush.* New York: Free Press, 2007.

Hoyle, Russ. *Going to War: How Misinformation, Disinformation, and Arrogance Led America into Iraq.* New York: Thomas Dunne Books, 2008.

Jacobson, Gary C. *A Divider, Not a Uniter: George W. Bush and the American People.* New York: Pearson Longman, 2008.

Kerry, John. *A Call to Service.* New York: Viking Press, 2003.

Kessler, Ronald. *Laura Bush: An Intimate Portrait of the First Lady.* New York: Doubleday, 2006.

Mansfield, Stephen. *The Faith of George W. Bush*. New York: Jeremy P. Tarcher/Penguin, 2003.

Maranto, Robert, Tom Lansford, and Jeremy Johnson, eds. *Judging Bush*. Stanford, CA: Stanford University Press, 2009.

Mendell, David. *Obama: From Promise to Power*. New York: Amistad, 2007.

Minutaglio, Bill. *First Son: George W. Bush and the Bush Family Dynasty*. New York: Times Books, 1999.

Mitchell, Elizabeth. *W: Revenge of the Bush Dynasty*. New York: Hyperion, 2000.

Mueller, James E. *Towel Snapping the Press: Bush's Journey from Locker-room Antics to Message Control*. Lanham. MD: Rowman & Littlefield, 2006

Phillips, Kevin. *American Dynasty: Aristocracy, Fortune, and the Politics of Deceit in the House of Bush*. New York: Viking Press, 2004.

Sanger, David. *The Inheritance: The World Obama Confronts and the Challenges to American Power*. New York: Harmony Books, 2009

Suskind, Ron. *The Price of Loyalty*. New York: Simon & Schuster, 2006.

Woodward, Bob. *Bush at War*. New York: Simon & Schuster, 2002.

———. *Plan of Attack*. New York: Simon & Schuster, 2004.

———. *State of Denial*. New York: Simon & Schuster, 2006.

———. *The War Within: A Secret White House History* 2006–2008. New York: Simon & Schuster, 2008.

Articles

Alexander, Paul. "All Hat, No Cattle." *Rolling Stone*, 5 August 1999. Available online at www.rollingstone.com/politics/story/6482734/all_hat_no_cattle. Accessed on 9 October 2009.

"Al Gore, Part III," Online NewsHour, 17 August 2000. Available online at www.pbs.org/newshour/election2000/demconvention/gore3.html. Accessed on 22 October 2009.

Allen, Mike. "Bush Unveils Mortgage Crisis First Steps," *Politico*, 31 August, 2007. Available online at www.politico.com/news/stories/0807/5581.html. Accessed on 1 December 2009.

Bronner, Ethan. "Governor Bush and Education; Turnaround in Texas Schools Looks Good for Bush in 2000." *The New York Times*, 28 May 1999. Available online at www.nytimes.com/1999/05/28/us/record-governor-bush-education-turnaround-texas-schools-looks-good-for-bush-2000.html?pagewanted=1. Accessed on 21 October 2009.

"Bush: 'I Will Give It My All,'" *The Guardian*, 14 December 2000. Available online at www.guardian.co.uk/world/2000/dec/14/uselections2000.usa13. Accessed on 22 October 2009.

"Bush: 'I'm the Decider' on Rumsfeld," CNN, 18 April 2006. Available online at www.cnn.com/2006/POLITICS/04/18/rumsfeld/. Accessed on 1 December 2009.

"Bush: U.S. Military on 'High Alert,'" CNN, 12 September 2001. Available online at http://archives.cnn.com/2001/US/09/11/bush.second.statement. Accessed on 12 October 2009.

"Bush's Environmental Record," Online NewsHour, 22 August 2000. Available online at www.pbs.org/newshour/bb/election/july-dec00/bush_environment_8-22.html. Accessed on 20 October 2009.

"'Can I Quit Now?' FEMA Chief Wrote as Katrina Raged," CNN, 3 November 2005. Available online at www.cnn.com/2005/US/11/03/brown.fema.emails/. Accessed on 9 November 2009.

Conason, Joe. "Notes on a Native Son." *Harper's Magazine*, February 2000, pp. 39–53.

Davis, Richard H. "The Anatomy of a Smear Campaign." *Boston Globe*, 21 March 2004. Available online at www.boston.com/news/globe/editorial_opinion/oped/articles/2004/03/21/the_anatomy_of_a_smear_campaign/. Accessed on 22 October 2009.

Duffy, Michael, and Nancy Gibbs. "The Quiet Dynasty." *Time*, 7 August 2000. Available online at www.time.com/time/magazine/article/0,9171,997635,00.html. Accessed on 11 November 2009.

Fletcher, Michael A. "Bush Defends CIA's Clandestine Prisons," *Washington Post*, 8 November 2005. Available online at www.washingtonpost.com/wp-dyn/content/article/2005/11/07/AR2005110700637.html. Accessed on 9 November 2009.

"Gov. George W. Bush," Online NewsHour, 3 August 2000. Available online at www.pbs.org/newshour/election2000/gopconvention/george_w_bush.html. Accessed on 22 October 2009.

Hess, Pamela. "Report: Bush Surveillance Program Was Massive." ABC News, 10 July 2009. Available online at http://abcnews.go.com/Politics/wireStory?id=8052894. Accessed on 10 July 2009.

Holguin, Jaime. "Bush Deficit Plan Draws Derision," CBS News, 17 December 2003. Available online at www.cbsnews.com/stories/2003/12/17/politics/main589170.shtml. Accessed on 27 October 2009.

Horowitz, David. "'I'm a Uniter, Not a Divider.'" *Salon*, 6 May 1999. Available online at www.salon.com/news/feature/1999/05/06/bush/. Accessed on 22 October 2009.

"In His Own Words: 'Leadership Comes in All Forms,' *Washington Post*, 27 July 1999. Available online at www.washingtonpost.com/wp-srv/politics/campaigns/wh2000/stories/bushtext072799.htm. Accessed on 14 October 2009.

Kinsley, Michael. "The Bush Presidency, Eight Years Later." *Time*, 31 December 2008. Available online at www.time.com/time/magazine/article/0,9171,1869213,00.html. Accessed on 30 November 2009.

Kranrich, Nancy. "The Impact of the USA PATRIOT Act: An Update." The Free Expression Policy Project, 27 August 2003. Available online at www.fepproject.org/commentaries/patriotactupdate.html. Accessed on 10 November 2009.

Kristoff, Nicholas D. "Ally of an Older Generation Amid the Tumult of the '60s," *The New York Times*, 19 June 2000. Available online at www.nytimes.com/library/politics/camp/061900wh-bush.html. Accessed on 13 October 2009.

———. "For Bush, Thrill Was in Father's Chase," *The New York Times*, 29 August 2000. Available online at www.nytimes.com/library/politics/camp/082900wh-bush.html. Accessed on 19 October 2009.

———. "Learning How to Run: A West Texas Stumble," *The New York Times*, 27 July 2000. Available online at www.nytimes.com/library/politics/camp/072700wh-bush-lubbock.html. Accessed on 16 October 2009.

Lardner, George Jr., and Lois Romano. "At Height of Vietnam, Bush Picks Guard," *Washington Post*, 28 July 1999. Available online at www.washingtonpost.com/wp-srv/politics/campaigns/wh2000/stories/bush072899.htm. Accessed on 14 October 2009.

———. "Bush Moves Up to the Majors," *Washington Post*, 31 July 1999. Available online at www.washingtonpost.com/wp-srv/politics/campaigns/wh2000/stories/bush073199.htm. Accessed on 19 October 2009.

———. "Bush Name Helps Fuel Oil Dealings," *Washington Post*, 30 July 1999. Available online at www.washingtonpost.com/wp-srv/politics/campaigns/wh2000/stories/bush073099.htm. Accessed on 16 October 2009.

———. "Young Bush, a Political Natural, Revs Up," *Washington Post*, 29 July 1999. Available online at www.washingtonpost.com/wp-srv/politics/campaigns/wh2000/stories/bush072999.htm. Accessed on 16 October 2009.

Milbank, Dana. "On a Bicycle in Beltsville, Blissfully Unaware," *Washington Post*, 12 May 2005. Available online at www.washingtonpost.com/wp-dyn/content/article/2005/05/11/AR2005051102170.html. Accessed on 9 November 2009.

Phillips, Kevin. "The Prospect of a Bush Restoration." *Harper's Magazine*, February 2000, pp. 54–58.

Priest, Dana. "CIA Holds Terror Suspects in Secret Prisons." *Washington Post*, 2 November 2005. Available online at www.washingtonpost. com/wp-dyn/content/article/2005/11/01/AR2005110101644.html. Accessed on 9 November 2009.

"Protesting the War," Online NewsHour, 26 September 2005. Available online at www.pbs.org/newshour/bb/military/july-dec05/ protests_9-26.html. Accessed on 10 November 2009.

Solomon, John. "Bush, Harvard Business School and the Makings of a President," *The New York Times*, 18 June 2000. Available online at www.nytimes.com/2000/06/18/business/bush-harvard-business-school-and-the-makings-of-a-president.html?pagewanted=2. Accessed on 15 October 2009.

Steinberg James B., Michael E. O'Hanlon, and Susan E. Rice. *The New National Security Strategy and Preemption*. Brookings Institute Policy Brief Series #113, December 2002. Available online at www.brookings.edu/ papers/2002/12terrorism_ohanlon.aspx. Accessed on 26 October 2009.

Steinhauser, Paul. "Most See Bush Presidency as a Failure, Polls Show." CNN, 18 January 2009. Available online at www.cnn.com/2009/ POLITICS/01/18/poll.bush.presidency. Accessed on 2 December 2009.

"Study: Bush, Aides Made 935 False Statements in Run-up to War." CNN, 24 January 2008. Available online at www.cnn.com/2008/ POLITICS/01/23/bush.iraq. Accessed on 26 October 2009.

Suellentrop, Chris. "America's New Political Capital," *Slate*, 30 November 2004. Available online at www.slate.com/id/2110256. Accessed on 9 November 2009.

"The Bush Record," *Sierra*, September/October 2004. Available online at www.sierraclub.org/sierra/200409/bush_record_print.asp. Accessed on 23 October 2009.

Thomas, Jo. "After Yale, Bush Ambled Amiably Into His Future," *The New York Times*, 22 July 2000. Available online at www.nytimes.com/library/politics/camp/072200wh-bush.html. Accessed on 14 October 2009.

"Transcript for February 8," *Meet the Press*, 13 February 2004. Available online at www.msnbc.msn.com/id/4179618/. Accessed on 13 October 2009.

Unger, Craig. "Battle of the Bushes." *Salon*, 7 November 2007. Available online at www.salon.com/books/feature/2007/11/07/house_of_bush/. Accessed on 22 October 2009.

Verhovek, Sam Howe. "Governor and Her Rival Meet in Debate," *The New York Times*, 22 October 1994. Available online at www.nytimes.com/1994/10/22/us/the-1994-campaign-texas-governor-and-her-rival-meet-in-debate.html> Accessed on 20 October 2009.

Williams, Grant. "The Bush Brand of Charity," *The Chronicle of Philanthropy*, 6 April 2000. Available online at http://philanthropy.com/free/articles/v12/i12/12000101.htm. Accessed on 21 October 2009.

Zakaria, Tabassum. "Bush Says If Younger, He Would Work in Afghanistan," Reuters, 13 March, 2008. Available online at www.reuters.com/article/idUSN1333111120080313. Accessed on 2 December 2009.

WEBSITES

The American Presidency Project

www.presidency.ucsb.edu/index_docs.php

Bush Presidency

www.cbsnews.com/htdocs/politics/bush/framesource.html

CNN

www.cnn.com

Commission on Presidential Debates

www.debates.org/

Frontline—The Choice 2000

www.pbs.org/wgbh/pages/frontline/shows/choice2000/bush/cron.html

The 9/11 Commission Report, National Commission on Terrorist Attacks upon the United States.

http://govinfo.library.unt.edu/911/report/index.htm

U.S.–Iraq War

http://usiraq.procon.org/

U.S. War in Afghanistan

www.cfr.org/publication/20018/

INDEX

Pages in **boldface** are illustrations.

★ ★ ★ ★ ★ ★ ★ ★ ★ ★ ★ ★ ★ ★ ★ ★ ★ ★ ★

★ ★ ★ ★ ★ ★ ★ ★ ★ ★ ★ ★ ★ ★ ★ ★ ★ ★ ★ ★

ABOUT THE AUTHOR

A history graduate of the University of Connecticut, freelance author Michael Burgan has written more than 150 fiction and nonfiction books for children, as well as articles for adults. He has written several books on World War II, the cold war, and U.S foreign policy. Burgan is a recipient of an Educational Press Association of America award.

★ ★ ★ ★ ★ ★ ★ ★ ★ ★ ★ ★ ★ ★ ★ ★ ★